Farwell

'79

The Encourager

The Encourager

Periodical Essays
by

D. Elton Trueblood

BROADMAN PRESS
Nashville, Tennessee

Dewey Decimal Classification: 248.4
Subject heading: CHRISTIAN LIFE
Library of Congress Catalog Card Number: 78–062527
Printed in the United States of America

Contents

118772

Introduction

Long ago I discovered that no person, no matter how dedicated, can accomplish much by working alone. Accordingly I have, for many years, carefully built a cadre of Christian workers, most of whom rejoice in the biblical term *Yokefellows*. Though this term was employed by Dwight L. Moody one hundred years ago, its contemporary use began in 1949 with a sermon I preached called "The Yoke of Christ," first delivered at Cleveland, Ohio, in May of that year. In rapid succession there emerged the use of the yoke pin as a means of witness; the cultivation of small groups, including those in factories and colleges; the creation of fellowships within prisons; the establishment of retreat centers; and, finally, the Yokefellow Academy, devoted to lay theological education.

Those who gladly call themselves Yokefellows are the men and women who, regardless of denominational affiliation or lack of it, envisage the Christian faith as something in which they have been personally recruited as workers. A genuine Christian is one, they believe, who is committed to Christ and who, accordingly, seeks to respond positively with his total life as he hears Christ's clearest call to commitment, "Take my yoke upon you" (Matt. 11:29). Since Christ requires participation in the work of a team, it becomes obvious that nominal or merely ceremonial Christianity is out of the question. Furthermore, genuine Christians are necessarily yoked with one another if they are yoked with Christ. It is required of the committed that they be joined together in a *company*. That an early Christian should address another follower of Christ as "true yoke–fellow" (Phil. 4:3) is neither strange nor esoteric but eminently reasonable.

It is fortunate that Yokefellows, in the modern sense, have never compiled a list of members. In a conscious effort to avoid even the appearance of competition with the churches, the emphasis has been placed on making Christians better members where they already belong. The happy alternative to membership has been that of *correspondence*. The major correspondence has involved the production of a letter four times a year. It is sent without remuneration to all who ask to have their names placed upon the mailing list.

When the first quarterly letters were written twenty years ago, they were little more than newsletters, intended to inform recipients about the doings of one another. This was the right strategy because it strengthened what was then a very small movement. Even then, however, there were suggestions of the pattern to be developed later. For example, the letter for June 1960 was entitled "The Yoke and the Plow" and included the following:

> We may be helped by Christ's figure of the plow. Undoubtedly the major use of the yoke, in his experience, was that of enabling animals to pull a plow through the earth. The apostle whom Christ calls is one who puts his hand to the plow; he is a mover of the earth. The old organization of United Presbyterian Men was so impressed with this figure that they designed a lapel button in the shape of a plow and wore it

for a few years. It was a good idea and one that could profitably be revived. The lesson of the plowers is that we dare not look back and we dare not look merely within. We must look forward. A movement that is not changing and developing is already dead. The one thing men cannot do is to perform a successful holding operation.

Beginning in 1968 something totally different began to emerge—a series of periodical essays devoted to problems about which people were perplexed. It is only this later phase that is represented in the present volume now produced at the gracious invitation of Broadman Press. Accordingly, all of the essays that follow have been written since my retirement from the philosophy professorship at Earlham College. My freedom from regular teaching has enabled me to give my undivided attention to what is really a new chapter of my life.

Because there is nothing else in which the widely scattered Yokefellows share, the quarterly letter has come to be the only uniting factor in the entire movement. I write the letters with a strong sense of responsibility, not as an isolated individual but as president of Yokefellows International. The epistolary form has served our purpose well because each printed letter leads to subsequent dialogue as people feel free to respond with both questions and suggestions of new topics. The epistolary pattern has therefore been far more than a literacy device. It is an explicit invitation to participation in dialogue, which is one of the chief means by which thinking proceeds. As the essays now appear in book form, all readers are invited to participate by writing to the office of Yokefellows International.

The essays collected in this volume were produced in conscious adherence to the tradition of English letters represented by Joseph Addison, Sir Richard Steele, and Dr. Samuel Johnson. The intention has been to demonstrate the possibility of what has come to be known as the compressed style. The best literature, I believe, is that which avoids both the verbose and the superfluous. When I entered upon my own literary career, I saw that many otherwise valuable literary productions are harmed by being padded; and I made a conscious effort to avoid this mistake. I believed then and believe now that important ideas can be expressed with brevity, providing the writer seeks to express them without jargon, employing the language that ordinary thoughtful people are able both to use and to understand. The decision to present the essays not in topical clusters but in the order in which they were written means that we are attempting another form of autobiography. The sensitive reader can envisage the growth of ideas as they have developed, step by step, in one particular mind which has been stimulated by other minds.

It is a great privilege to be a human being. To be human is to share in both tragedy and wonder, and we can never express adequately the depth of either of these. One of the most exciting of human facts is that persons are able to stimulate each other in productive ways. When two persons, formerly strangers, are brought together, the effect is always unpredictable and sometimes revolutionary. Though each may have been relatively unproductive alone, the combination may be amazing. One person of modest powers may ignite another of equally modest powers so that the outcome is something which no one could possibly have predicted. This is an illustration, on the highest level of experience, of the phenomenon called *emergence*, which appears in many different forms. Except in the abstraction called mathematics, the whole is always greater than the sum of its parts.

As I look at the remainder of my life, I know that I want to use much of it in bringing together people who need one another but who cannot possibly be aware of what their exact need is. One of the crucial experiences in my life, as a good many of my readers know, is my long exposure to the thinking and literary style of Dr. Samuel Johnson. Johnson was a great writer, but he was even greater as a person. The strangest development of his personality came about through one of the oddest friendships of history, that between the great man of literature and the bumptious young Scottish lawyer James Boswell. Since Boswell later produced what is generally recognized as the finest biography of the world, the friendship was incalculably profitable for both men. We should not know Johnson nearly so well were it not for the keen perception of the younger man; and Boswell would not be remembered at all had not the wise scholar brought out the best of his talent.

The strange meeting of Johnson and Boswell occurred in 1763, in the back parlor of Tom Davies' bookshop on Great Russell Street, London. Davies, of course, was doing more for literature than he could possibly have supposed. Johnson was fifty-three; his reputation was already established; the *Dictionary* had been published; and all issues of the *Rambler*, the *Adventurer*, and the *Idler* were behind him. His literary dictatorship was unchallenged. By contrast, Boswell had accomplished virtually nothing. But the odd combination worked because each brought out something significant in the other. It is a present fact and not merely an antique proverb that iron sharpens iron.

Not one of us involved in this particular correspondence is likely to become either a Johnson or a Boswell, but we may nevertheless have our own counterparts of the meeting in the bookshop on Great Russell Street. Our major undertaking can be that of trying to bring out the best in each person whom we are able to meet. It is common knowledge that some people bring out the best that is in us, while others bring out the worst. One mark of Christian character is the ability to make another see in himself something which formerly he little suspected.

"Those who attempt periodical essays seem to be often stopped in the beginning, by the difficulty of finding a proper title," wrote Samuel Johnson as he began the first *Idler* on April 15, 1758. Now, 220 years later, I have the same difficulty. Having no expectation that these periodical essays would ever appear in book form, I have not needed a title. My only purpose has been to put into intelligible prose what has seemed worth saying to people who are both thoughtful and devout.

It is perhaps true that no title is ever wholly satisfactory. Certainly the title *Rambler* did not express accurately who Samuel Johnson was, since he remained in London almost continuously while writing two essays a week from 1750 to 1752. For a man who worked so hard, *Idler* was not much better; and the *Spectator* always did more than observe. Recognizing that I am not likely to succeed in a search which has baffled the giants, I must nevertheless have a title of some kind.

An ideal title is competent to denote what the essential purpose of a literary production is. As I have tried to restate my own fundamental convictions about the faith to which I am committed, my concrete purpose has become increasingly clear. One of the most revolutionary ideas which has possessed me is the recognition that it is not possible to be a Christian *alone!*

Where there is no fellowship, there is no reality. Christians, I deeply believe, are called not to a separated righteousness but to a yoked existence in which each member of the team does more than pull his share of the load. He actually helps the others to pull better than they could in isolation.

With this philosophy of the Christian faith in mind, I have asked seriously what my own vocation is. By training and by toil I have, I believe, been prepared to assist people in the clarification of their thinking. Today most Christians seem to feel the need of help at this particular point because there are puzzling developments wherever we look. Men and women need the encouragement which comes from the realization that the faith can be sustained with full examination. They are strengthened when they learn that it is possible for the committed Christian to be not only devout but also intellectually honest—able both to fortify his own position and to face fearlessly all opposition. He is encouraged when he knows that the faith is an anvil that has worn out many hammers. With such ideas uppermost in my mind, meditating upon the ways in which one life can build hope in another, it suddenly occurred to me that the only adequate word for what we mean is *Encourager.* This term, though novel, penetrates to the heart of the experience which the writers of the New Testament stressed when they employed the often-repeated phrase "one another."

Because *Encourager* is what I seek to be, I think of my *Letters* in personal terms. They are addressed to *persons!* Many years ago I chose, as my golden text, the injunction which, in the Revised Standard Version, is brilliantly translated, "Therefore encourage one another and build one another up" (1 Thess. 5:11). If the short periodical essays selected for reproduction in this volume have some part in the ministry of encouragement, I shall be satisfied, convinced that the labor of producing them, over a period of years, has been justified.

D. ELTON TRUEBLOOD

Earlham College
Easter 1978

1

Perplexity

June 1969

If I understand you aright, you are perplexed. I want you to know that I am likewise perplexed. There is so much in our world that is right, but it seems at the moment to be overshadowed by much that is wrong. There are many decent and fundamentally unselfish people who go about their work and try to keep the peace while they are engaged in works of mercy and justice, but they do not make as many headlines as do others. The Christian must always be a realist. He dare not comfort himself with delusions of any kind; and, consequently, he must not minimize the forces of evil.

I know that those who read this letter are eager to know what I think about the present situation in the colleges and universities. Naturally I think about the problem a great deal because most of my public career has been spent in these institutions. Much of what I see makes me very sad. I have to admit that violence appears to be successful; I have to admit that many of the professors and administrators are apparently spineless and are easily intimidated by a show of force. I want the black students to have every opportunity, but I am well aware that what is being done in many institutions is really a disservice to them. There is no reason to suppose that they will be helped perma-

15

nently by the segregation which they demand and now receive. There is no good reason to think that their problems will be solved by giving them cheap courses devoid of content. Such courses have the effect of reducing the value of the degree which is supposedly earned. What these students need is good teaching and hard courses, whether in English, mathematics, philosophy, science, or engineering. The black students need the kind of education which will enable them to compete in the public arena on a level of equality, and the lowering of standards will not have this effect.

Though there is much dissension among the students and a discouraging unwillingness to engage in rational discourse, the deeper malady is in the faculties. It is almost incredible that the American Association of University Professors should reject the argument of the Attorney General calling for equal treatment before the law. Though the professors professed to see in this a threat to academic freedom, what they demonstrate is confusion about the meaning of freedom. Teachers who are locked out of their lecture rooms are not thereby made more free. Unless there can be some protection for the majority against the tyranny of the minority there will not be freedom for anybody.

Always, as we move forward, we must fight on two fronts. The golden text of this double struggle may be found in the words of Christ when he bade us, "Beware of the leaven of the Pharisees, and of the leaven of Herod" (Mark 8:15). For us, in our time, the dual struggle is against the tyranny of both the right and the left. Sometimes one of these is the major danger and sometimes it is the other. In the ascendency of Mussolini the clearest danger was that of Fascism, which is simply another name for the danger on the right. In America this danger once appeared in the form represented by the Ku Klux Klan and by the cruel attacks of the late Sen. Joseph McCarthy, who made things so difficult for President Eisenhower. A strange fact now is that a good many people are still fighting old battles on the supposition that the major danger is still what it formerly was. It is part of our needed realism now—a realism in which commited Christians should take the lead—to point out that we are in a new day in which the major danger comes from the left. Any man is obsolete if he still thinks of the Ku Klux Klan as a threat, for it is now largely a joke; and it is a part of wisdom not to waste our time on what is insignificant or nonexistent. The new left, however, is a totally different matter. It is dangerous because it is well organized and utterly ruthless, having no moral position at all but only a thirst for power. The apostles of the new left are not in the least deterred by questions of honesty. There is no reason to suppose that they care about issues, for issues can always be invented. It is doubtful, for example, that the members of the Students for a Democratic Society had any sincere concern about a proposed new gymnasium at Columbia University. One of their chief leaders finally admitted that he did not even know what the proposed location was until after the fight had started.

One of the greatest dangers in facing the present threat to our liberty is that the people who are believers in freedom may be permissive to those who would destroy freedom. There is a tendency, especially in Christian circles, to believe that the violent ones are really well meaning and that if we could only meet them as persons, we and they would understand. Many who have believed this have been badly burned because they are met not with dialogue but with shouts.

Some people have taken comfort from the fact that the ones who are so violent now are not identical with the apostles of Hitlerism a third of a century ago. But this is extremely naive. What is the real difference between shouting "Ho Chi Minh" and "Heil Hitler"? The similarity is that of mood. The sounds are uttered with complete self-righteousness and with complete unwillingness to engage in dialogue. There is no reason whatever to think that if, by some miracle, the war in Vietnam can be honorably ended, these shouts will end. We are dealing with something very much like a religion which, because it is utterly ruthless, will be able to find new issues when old ones are eliminated.

I know that many of my readers are worried about the Supreme Court, and well they may be! The Supreme Court is very important to all of us because it stands at the apex of our legal system. Anything that undermines respect for the law is harmful to our total society. The present Supreme Court has made decisions which have the effect of undermining its authority and thus hurting everybody. Some of the decisions which protect the purveyors of the obscene are so strange that we find them difficult to understand. The same may be said of decisions which give real advantage to the criminal in the contests between him and innocent men and women. The only possible way to understand perverse decisions is that these men are guided by some strange ideology which makes them stretch the words of the Constitution, making applications which bear no real resemblance to what the founding fathers obviously intended. What kind of intellectual aberration must there be in any man's mind if he thinks that the First Amendment is meant to protect one who burns the flag? Now we have a new and deeper difficulty in that members of the Supreme Court have been found to be engaged in what are, at best, shady financial practices. Since the only real power of the Court is its moral power, we are, indeed, in a bad situation when this power is eroded by the personal conduct of those who are placed in a position to judge others.

What is happening in our time is really a verification of what Christians have long known, namely, that it is not possible to maintain a civilization which is severed from its spiritual roots. Certainly, we must report that the severance has largely occurred and that the consequent withering has come to pass. The colleges in which there is the most trouble today are the colleges in which it is believed that a secular society can be self-sufficient. For a generation we have seen the erosion of the Christian concept of the college, and this has been produced by those who have considered it as an emancipation. The demise of the required convocation in many institutions, including those with supposed church connection, is one of the most evident of the steps taken. Along with this has gone the refusal of college officials to take any responsibility for the moral training of the students. It is now clear to anyone who will observe it that this has been a fundamentally naive process. The chickens have come home to roost. The harvest of confusion and of evasion of responsibility has appeared.

We must never give up. The task of commited Christians is to roll back the tide. It is not new for the followers of Christ to face fierce and apparently successful antagonism. I hope that all who read this letter will turn with a new conviction to the eighth chapter of Romans, a chapter which helps us to keep up our courage in the face of difficulties and opposition. I am persuaded that neither violence nor noise nor manufactured confusion will be able to separate us from the love of God in Christ Jesus, our Lord.

2

Moon Walk

We can now consider in some perspective what was undoubtedly the most important event of this year and possibly the most important of our entire lives. The walk on the moon by two members of the crew of Apollo 11 and their subsequent safe return to the earth is something which it is impossible to overpraise. It is not really very surprising that even some of the hard-boiled reporters admitted that, at the start of this momentous voyage, conscious of the mood of reverence, they underwent what one of them has called a religious experience.

We are all filled with wonder when we realize the degree to which this astounding enterprise began and ended on time and the way in which so many of the intricate operations worked together in harmony. The whole thing makes us very proud, not merely of the fact that we are Americans, but that we are members of the human race. A new pattern has been created and created in such a way that it is clear that men are really made in God's image. With all our sin and foolishness, we have a certain kinship to almighty God because we can think his thoughts after him and take advantage of our partial knowledge of his laws to make enormous leaps into areas hitherto unknown and unfrequented.

21

We have been acutely conscious of the wonderful team-work which has been required. On the team have been the people who have made the delicate instruments, the highly trained persons in the control center in Houston, the members of the United States Navy who planned the recovery in the Pacific Ocean, and so many more. The success of the moon landing depended upon the work of artisans, scientists, engineers, architects, scholars, pilots, swimmers, photographers. Most of us will not forget the families of the three brave men who, more than any of the rest of us, had a stake in their safe return. There is no way of knowing how much prayer was offered up, but we can have some hint of it by getting the direct report of Commander Armstrong's mother.

One of the most wonderful things about the successful venture, which for the first time in history made it possible for human beings to set foot on a celestial body, was the way in which the operation seemed to be lacking in human conceit. The grandeur of the event made humble reverence seem amazingly right. Moreover, the magnitude of the undertaking has made it possible for most of us to avoid a merely national pride. The men who first set foot upon the moon were humans first, and Americans second. It is highly significant that among the records left behind on the moon's surface were reminders of Russian explorers in space. Indeed, as success came, it seemed less and less like a race between Russia and the United States.

Important as the landing on the moon may be in the increase in knowledge of celestial bodies, it seems likely that the event may have a still greater impact upon the morale of our people. It could even change the trend in moral fashions and especially the direction of the hippie way of life. It must be obvious to everyone who thinks about the matter that the astronauts are a threat to the hippies because these superb men represent all of the virtues which hippies affect to despise; and, furthermore, they succeeded. The astronauts are not dropouts! They combine hard work, self-discipline, trained intelligence, and marital fidelity. In short, they are squares! They shave; they are clean; they do not specialize in obscene language; they do not use drugs; they are not ashamed to be patriotic. Because these men are so admirable and because they cannot be dismissed as the establishment, it is wholly possible that they can present the upcoming generation with a new and effective ideal. They may do far more than they know to roll back the tide of permissiveness which has so threatened to engulf us. The fact that these men are, for the most part, reverent Christians will not be lost upon the young.

The very appearance of the members of the Apollo team may be expected to have a beneficent effect. Viewers of the TV presentation must have noticed, for example, that all of the men in Mission Control in Houston wear ties when on duty. There is much reason to conclude that sloppiness in dress has an effect upon both thought and action. It has, indeed, been one of the most damaging aspects of our recent cultural sickness.

You have probably noticed that many people have been quick to ask why it is not possible to apply to the problems of poverty or war or drug addiction the same fine-tuned efficiency which has been exhibited in the Apollo flights. Though there is no harm in asking this question, it is a serious mistake to suppose that the two sets of problems are comparable. However great the intelligence and dedication employed to make possible the successful outcome of an Apollo flight, the task is far easier than is any task

concerned primarily with human conduct. Many of the
elements are mechanical ones; and however intricate the
machines may be, they are nevertheless different in kind
from persons. They are not free agents; they do not make
decisions; they do not sin.

Frequently, when people complain that the social sciences are so much less developed than the physical sciences,
their complaint is really naive. It is naive because mention
is not made of the fact that physical things can be manipu-
lated, as persons cannot. If men and women were pawns,
so that they could be moved at will by planners, a highly
peaceful operation might be possible. But that is not how
it is, and we are glad that it is not that way. Much of
the complaint about the failure of humanity, as contrasted
with scientific enterprises, really depends upon nothing
more profound than a determinist philosophy of human
life. We cannot know, in our finitude, all that is true about
human life; but we can at least know that determinism
is a false philosophy. In any case it is utterly incompatible
with the Christian view of reality.

It is recognized, of course, that the successful Apollo
program included a number of people who had to work
together to make a success. But it must be noted that this
group, however large, was highly select and was made
up of people who were already strongly motivated and
disciplined when they entered the program. The same cannot be said when we seek to overcome human poverty.
Then, by the nature of the case, we deal with great numbers of people who do not really want to be helped. Some
are lazy, and others are corrupt. It is our task to try to
help these people all that we can by providing new motivation and new standards; but we cannot force people to
do what they do not want to do. Even if the social sciences

were subsidized with the same funds and could recruit at the same level of competence, as is the case with the physical sciences, there is no reason to think that the results would be comparable because we are dealing with persons far more than with things.

One of the great assets of the Christian faith is that it has always helped people to avoid becoming naive about the human situation. Basic Christianity, far from preaching natural human goodness, has always stressed the doctrine of original sin. By this, Christians mean the realistic recognition that sin is always potential in every human heart. It can appear in priests and in philosophers just as it appears in the rank and file of the population. It is not limited in regard to sex, race, or age. It is part of the human situation, Christianity teaches, that self-centeredness can enter at any level. Consequently we should never be complaisant, and we must not allow power to be used without some form of surveillance and control. All need forgiveness and all need grace. Consequently, the Christian, if he understands his own faith, is never utopian. Though he will do all that he can to help to make a better world, he realizes full well that, a thousand years from now, if there are people on the earth at that time, there will still be self-centeredness. It is the price of personhood.

Ennobling as the moon landing of the Apollo crewmen has been, we are still faced, and shall continue to be faced, with the hard problems of human life. I am personally grateful, as we face these, for the wisdom of the Christian faith, which provides us with such a delicate combination of realism and hope.

3

The Written Word

December 1969

Though we all read many current periodicals and books, frequently our attention is not directed to significant evidence of greatness through the written word. I refer specifically to the writings of William Barclay.

What is great about the contemporary Barclay is the man's amazing ability to interpret the Bible to modern men and women, without diluting, in any degree, his strong emphasis on the uniqueness of Christ. Barclay uses his powers of scholarship, including a brilliant understanding of the Greek language, to make the Bible mean more to anyone who is willing to read and to learn. In his commentaries, particularly those on Matthew and Mark, the Scottish scholar proves that it is possible to be accurate without being dull and to be pertinent without also being superficial. In his careful yet reverent treatment of the Apostles' Creed, he demonstrates the possibility of being tough-minded and tender-minded at the same time. Barclay combines, as do few persons in our age, the union of the clear head and the warm heart.

My reason for calling your attention to William Barclay is that I want to direct your energies, if I can, into deeper thinking about the meaning of the Christian faith. We are surrounded by neighbors who are deeply perplexed about what they ought to believe. It is the task of every one of us to give an answer to every person who asks about our central convictions (1 Pet. 3:15), but we need a great deal of help if we are to do this effectively. Whenever a man like Barclay appears, we rightly thank God for him because he helps us to have answers which would not occur to us operating merely upon our own resources. As head of the divinity school at Glasgow University, this man cares for his own students; but most of those whom he teaches are the thousands who, though he never sees them, are really his students because they read his many books.

The more I ponder, the more grateful I am for the written word. We can be helped today by the ideas of Karl Barth, C. S. Lewis, and many others, just as we were when they were still existing in the flesh. The spoken word is powerful, but the written word is more powerful because it bridges the chasms of both time and space.

Every man or woman who receives this letter is one who has a potential ministry in reaching other men and women involved in common life. Each stands on a front line where the problems are. What are you going to say? What can you say to your neighbor or your acquaintance who has just found that he has a terminal illness? What will you say to one who says he cannot believe in God because God, if he really existed, would not allow wars to occur? It is not enough for you to say, "Go see my pastor." In the first place, he probably will not go. And in the second place, he might listen more attentively to one who is already his friend and personal associate. The answer must be given when it is requested.

It is amazing to note how many people seem unable to interpret the Christian faith in rational terms. They are baffled by expressions which they do not understand and simply give up. For example, many seem baffled by the Apostles' Creed and finally dismiss it as obsolete. As a matter of fact, each item in it can be defended intelligently, provided we take the trouble to understand. William Barclay helps me, in this connection, in reference to the expression "He descended into hell." In some congregations this statement is considered so baffling that it is actually omitted when the Creed is repeated. But Barclay makes me understand that this is a vivid way of saying that Christ really died. His death on the cross was not illusory but real. There was no deception! He really died, says the Christian faith, and he really rose again. The Creed directs us to a hard realism. I cannot exaggerate the help which came to my mind when I was made to see this. It is an illustration of the way in which men can be helpful to one another.

Another problem of rational faith which may bother some who read these words centers on the "resurrection of the body." Many find this puzzling because they suppose it refers to the flesh which we now utilize. But this is not the case at all. What is referred to is a new "spiritual body," a paradoxical expression indicating "a means of individual identification." The physical body, which will decay, serves this purpose now. And we have reason to believe that God will provide another means of identification when we are liberated from the flesh with all of its limitations and pains.

To think that these physical bodies will go on forever is completely unsatisfactory. It is unsatisfactory for many reasons, one of the most convincing being that such a situation would perpetuate injustice. The hunchback would be a hunchback forever. Christ's clear teaching is to the contrary. God, in his infinite wisdom, will not give up on us just because the heart stops beating. We cannot know what a spiritual body can be because we are operating under finite limitations. But we can be sure that, though different, it will be more wonderful than anything we can know or dream.

For those who are seriously troubled about the resurrection of the body I recommend a careful study of 1 Corinthians, chapter 15. This is not as well known as the thirteenth chapter of the same book, but it is equally glorious. See especially verse 44, "It is sown a natural body; it is raised a spiritual body. There is a natural body, and there is a spiritual body." This will help you see that a great idea must not be dismissed merely because it is difficult to comprehend. We are called to greater thinking in order that we may help to clarify the thinking of others. If you can take away the barriers to faith in some person's mind, you are performing a genuine service.

This is a great time to be a Christian. We are in a great age which is not made less great by the fact that it presents serious problems. This is, potentially, one of the noblest periods of the Christian faith. Let us try to be worthy of it.

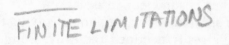

4

Dark Days

March 1970

When we try to be honest we have to admit that, in some ways, the church of Christ is going through dark days. Many devout people are clearly discouraged, the reasons for discouragement being fairly obvious. First of all, there is, in the church, a sharp division marked by mutual distrust. The new division has nothing to do with denominational rivalry, which is essentially a thing of the past, but occurs within denominations and within individual congregations. As I travel I hear of more distrust than I have encountered in many years. The worst distrust occurs between what may accurately be termed parties. One such party is devoted to protests and marches, while the opposite party is devoted to prayer and personal evangelism. The sorrowful fact is that each party is missing something greatly needed, even when there is a stress upon something that is valuable. Though both devotion and service are necessary, neither is sufficient in isolation.

One result of sharp division is financial, giving to church budgets having already declined radically. Congregations who have rejoiced in increasing budgets for a decade now find that they are forced to retrench. The major reason for this is not that people are without funds or that they are ungenerous. It is, rather, that great numbers are convinced that their money is being used for purposes of which they simply do not approve. This is especially so when it appears to people that their money is being handed over uncritically to movements that foster violence. The problem is accentuated when some prominent church leaders actually announce their support of violence as a method of social change.

Another reason for discouragement is the loss of pastoral leadership. I personally know of a number of congregations in which it seems to be almost impossible to secure the services of a high-caliber pastor. Many pastors have become so discouraged that they have accepted secular employment with evident relief. At the same time, it is increasingly difficult to enlist the ablest young men in training for the pastoral ministry.

It is in the light of contemporary discouragement that our function as Yokefellows becomes increasingly clear. The yoke is a way of binding together the separate parts which are impotent in separation. We have been led to adopt a philosophy that stresses equally both devotion and compassion, both worship and work, both mind and heart. We believe that the warm heart and the clear mind, far from being separate options, require one another. With the apostle Paul every Yokefellow can truly say, "I will pray with the spirit, and I will pray with the understanding also" (1 Cor. 14:15).

Perhaps it is in regard to the erosion of the professional ministry that our emphasis can be most redemptive at this particular juncture. While we have long seen the necessity of the ministry, we have never supposed that it is limited to a professional class. It is possible that some congregations may find that their very inability to secure professional ministerial leadership may turn out to be a surprising asset. It is almost certain to be an asset if the ordinary members, in spite of their involvement in secular pursuits, begin to contribute more than money and to function as more than members of the audience. What looks like misfortune may turn out, if faced rightly, to be a means of grace and even of growth.

As the number of available full-time pastors diminishes, we must find new resources. Some leaders, when funds are scarce, emulate Paul by instituting a modern equivalent of tent making. It is not unreasonable for a man with a strong sense of call to the ministry to consider joining a local police force or a fire department. Such jobs certainly place men where the need is, and they take away all suggestion of retiring to an ivory tower.

The opposite movement, that which comes when persons already employed in secular occupations give themselves more and more to the ministry of both evangelism and service, must go forward at the same time. One of the most hopeful sources of this new ministry is the body of men and women who receive this particular letter by virtue of being on the regular Yokefellow mailing list. Will you, therefore, as you read this letter, begin to examine your own witness? Are you willing to prepare and to give a sermon when opportunity offers? Or will you refuse, using the obsolete excuse that you are not a preacher? We have made a step forward in our understanding of the gospel when we recognize that each Christian must be a preacher in one way or another. Whatever it is that you are not willing to share is something that you do not really prize!

One reason why we need to form small sharing groups is that we can thereby receive help from one another in preparation for our own personal ministry. The truth is that each of us, far from being self-sufficient, needs all of the help that he can get. Our abilities are modest, but even modest abilities may be magnified by the experience of sharing. Also, each needs to make his ministry a matter of prayer. You can start every day by asking and listening for an answer, with words something like these: "Lord, what ministry do you have for me to perform today?"

However dark our time may be and however divided the church may be, committed Christians never despair. We do not despair because there is good reason to believe that God will revive the church in our time as he has revived it in other and even more desperate times. A movement which has borne the brunt of Roman persecution and intellectual contempt will be able to bear any attacks that may be leveled at it today. One of the best verified of historical predictions is that the powers of death will not be able to prevail (Matt. 16:18). We, like Peter, seem poor stuff on which to build Christ's church, but the miracle of history is that Christ can make use of our kind of rubble. Do not listen to foolish talk about the days of the church being already ended. It is not true!

5

Jesus People

December 1971

As I speak around the country these days, there is often a question period; and the first question asked is highly predictable. In almost every place, someone asks, "What do you think of the Jesus people?" The repetition of this query, along with the obvious sincerity of those who ask it, has made me approach the current phenomenon with all the care I can muster.

The new people calling themselves the "Jesus people" and termed by their detractors "Jesus freaks" have sprung up with apparent spontaneity in many different parts of our country in the last few months. Characteristically, the adherents of the new movement are relatively young people who have been part of the drug culture against which they have revolted after they have seen that drugs are unable to meet any fundamental human needs. In a mood of desperation they have turned to Jesus as a viable alternative to their former despair and disillusionment. In their commitment to Jesus, many seem to have discovered a new way of ordering their emotions as well as liberation from the bondage of both compulsive drug use and obsession with sex.

The new life in which these people now rejoice is one of almost continuous hilarity. They shout and sing and call out to anyone who will listen, "Jesus loves you." As is not very surprising, they often retain some of the external marks of their former way of life, including long hair and strict conformity in dress. While adopting a new gospel, they retain the appearance and many of the manners of hippies. This paradox is responsible for much of the attention accorded them by the news media. They are bound to make news in a way which neither the conventional hippie nor the conventional Christian make it.

Now what is the right reaction of a committed Christian to this phenomenon? Obviously, when we think about it with any seriousness, we cannot give an easy and simple answer, either of approbation or rejection. Because the situation is complex, we are required to form a complex answer! Though no one can know the answer perfectly, some relevant points are as follows:

In the first place, we must be glad when anyone turns from self-destruction to fulfillment. Drugs are bound to be harmful even when they do not cause actual brain damage. They are harmful because they encourage escape from reality, cheating those who turn to them by not providing what they seem to provide. And, far from giving real answers to any problem, they make the search for an answer even more difficult. We do not know much about life, but we at least know that the good life comes not by evading difficulties but by facing them.

The adherents of the new cult often carry about with them tattered copies of the New Testament which they read assiduously. This is clearly a tremendous gain over the nothingness which may have been experienced formerly. Any seeker who daily confronts Christ, as revealed in the Gospels, is almost sure to become a better person. There may, unfortunately, be no understanding of the scholarly work on the Gospels which has been undertaken for more than a hundred years; and there may be no recognition of literary sources. But the captivating figure of Jesus is almost bound to emerge as a force for good. Just to know intimately what Jesus said and did, including the way in which he died and rose again, is to know something of a revolutionary importance. One does not have to be a scholar or acquire a mastery of Greek to feel the attraction of the character of Jesus.

At the same time that we recognize the positive value of the central experience of concentrating upon Jesus, we must be sufficiently clear-minded to recognize the dangers and shortcomings of what is a fundamentally simplistic approach. The chief weaknesses of the new cult are four.

One weakness is that the Jesus people do not represent a full gospel. However valuable it may be to concentrate upon Christ, there are other aspects of truth which are needed. How strange, for example, to have so little reference to God! After all, Christ claimed to reveal the Father and to point people beyond himself to the one whom he addressed as "Lord of heaven and earth." Christ prayed, and he certainly did not pray to himself. The weakness of the new cult in this important detail is made vivid by the recognition that it is really a new Unitarianism. It is just as truly Unitarian to place the exclusive emphasis upon Jesus as it is, in the old-fashioned Unitarianism, to put the exclusive emphasis upon God. The important point to make is that it is always a mistake to deny the fullness of the gospel.

A second weakness of the new cult is its almost total lack of intellectual content. The emphasis is on raw emotion. No religion can continue very long in this condition of precarious imbalance. Many religions have begun with an emotional surge; but they have died, one by one, unless they have been able to add the element of intellectual validity, comparable to that which Robert Barclay added to original Quakerism. There is every reason to believe that seventeenth-century Quaker enthusiasm would have died, as did similar movements, if it had not received the strong intellectual support of men of the character of Barclay and Penn. The Jesus movement of our generation may eventually generate some kind of intellectual structure. But, if it cannot be so, it will probably achieve only temporary significance. Sooner or later it is necessary for all Christians to be able to give answers to anyone who asks about the hope that sustains them (1 Pet. 3:15).

A third weakness of the new cult is its separation from and antagonism to the church. No one who is reasonably aware of contemporary events can find it very difficult to see why vital new movements are often antichurch. This is because some churches seem to have become mere organizations, intent upon their own survival. They tend in the same direction as that followed by both the Temple and the synagogue which Jesus transcended. It is always helpful to read his searching words "Something greater than the temple is here" (Matt. 12:6, RSV). But having understood the reasons for the rejection of the church, we must go on to recognize that there cannot, in the long run, be any Christianity at all without it. Bad as the church may be, the world without it is worse! Apart from the church, with all of its mistakes, the new "people" would never have been able even to hear the name of Jesus. It is the continuing fellowship of inadequate men and women which perpetuates the gospel in the world. The new movement, therefore, will necessarily join the church which exists or else try to create one of its own.

A final weakness of the Jesus people is their relative lack of a social gospel. Their expression of the faith of Christ is too subjective, centering almost wholly upon a warm glow in the heart of the person who is committed to the newly discovered alternative to despair. Because there is an evangelistic emphasis, the new religion cannot rightly be called entirely self-centered; but what is lacking is any concerted effort to alter social structures. How, for example, can the movement, as now experienced, make any real difference in regard to either racial discrimination or poverty? A genuine gospel will always be concerned with human justice rather than the mere cultivation of a warm inner glow. Conceivably, the movement may be able, in the near future, to involve a social witness, as it may be able to involve intellectual support. But there is no evidence that it has yet done so.

Though it is possible that a fragmented gospel is preferable to none at all, there is no doubt where our own emphasis must lie. We must seek to hold aloft the vision of wholeness and to be always unsatisfied with any message which falls short of this vision. We are called upon to be both tender-minded and tough-minded and to be both at once.

6

Second Coming

June 1972

Because contemporary Christians are called to think as well as to act, we must help each other to be clear on subjects which are uppermost in the public mind. Several of the subjects which enormously interest devout people are highly perplexing ones. Prominent among these are the Jesus people, of whom I wrote to you six months ago, and the second coming of Christ. The present letter is devoted exclusively to the latter subject.

There are several reasons why the idea of a second coming is appealing to contemporary men and women. One reason is that people are deeply discouraged about human efforts at improvement. Each social dream turns out to be disappointing. The organization of United Nations twenty-seven years ago, seemed, for a while, to insure peace in our time; but it was soon obvious that it was only minimal in its effect. Today millions have lost moral respect for it. The same is true of other social devices. We obviously go on with human strife, regardless of change in economic or political systems. Even religion, instead of ending strife, sometimes increases it! This is true not only when the adversaries are Arabs and Jews, as in the Middle East, but even when both parties are Christians, as in Ireland.

The old belief in human perfectibility has lost, so far

as contemporary thinking man is concerned, nearly all of its credibility. The heady idealism of the earlier social gospel seems particularly dated today, since the dreams have simply not come to pass. Once we sang, with straight faces, "These things shall be: a loftier race/Than e're the world hath known shall rise"; but who can sing these naive words today? The perfectibility of human institutions by human effort, as popularized by French thinkers of the eighteenth century, cannot possibly be grafted onto an intelligent Christianity because it is incompatible with the Christian recognition of the chronic character of sin. Part of the realism of the gospel consists of the recognition that sin will appear, even in the most idealistic of religious efforts. After all, Christ was opposed by the religious establishment.

The simple truth is that nearly all thoughtful Christians have abandoned the once-popular idea that we can establish the kingdom of God on earth by our own efforts. Though we recognize the evil of both war and poverty, we are not able to eliminate either one of these; and there seems to be no trick by which we can succeed in doing so. We are beginning to take seriously the words of Christ, "You always have the poor with you" (Mark 14:7, RSV). Christ's words about the permanence of poverty were essentially a quotation from Deuteronomy 15:11, "The poor will never cease out of the land" (RSV). The thoughtful Christian will do his best to liberate other men from various endemic dangers; but, insofar as he understands Christ, he will not be simpleminded about his expectations of complete success.

In the light of the growth of Christian realism about the human predicament, the widespread interest in the second coming is increasingly clear. Sincere Christians

pray, as Christ taught them to pray, "Thy kingdom come
. . . on earth" (RSV). But they see, almost universally,
that the only genuine answer to the prayer will have to
be a special act of God because it certainly will not be
our own. Modern man sees that, if ever there is to be a
world of perfect love and justice, it will have to be God's
own doing since it clearly is not within man's power to
accomplish. In a profound sense, the emphasis upon the
second coming is necessary if hope is to have a reasonable
basis. This conclusion is wonderfully independent of
changes in culture or the advances of science. Unless God
intervenes in the historical order we can expect to have
most of the troubles we now experience a thousand years
hence. This is true because the troubles arise in the human
heart. The chief reason why science will not become a
panacea is that science is never independent of scientists,
and scientists are fallible men like the rest of us.

A second reason for the resurgence of interest in the
second coming is our new emphasis on Christ. No serious
reader of the Gospels can escape the fact that Christ had
so much to say about a return of the Son of Man. Nearly
all of the thirteenth chapter of Mark's Gospel is devoted
to this important subject. Central to the discourse are the
words "In those days, after that tribulation, the sun will
be darkened, and the moon will not give its light, and
the stars will be falling from heaven, and the powers in
the heavens will be shaken. And then they will see the
Son of man coming in clouds with great power and glory.
And then he will send out the angels, and gather his elect
from the four winds, from the ends of the earth to the
ends of heaven" (Mark 13:24–27, RSV).

Anyone who proposes to take Christ seriously must
reckon with these amazing words. Part of the problem

arises from the fact that such an event did not occur in a literal sense and has not yet occurred. The stars have not fallen, and nearly two thousand years of history have intervened between the time when the words were spoken and the present. It is possible, of course, that the events mentioned may yet occur, even in our own time, but are out of the reach of our understanding. It is hard to see how a sincere Christian could deny the possibility of an end to history as we know it, for a Christian believes, with Christ, that "all things are possible with God" (Mark 10:27, RSV).

The major task of a thoughtful Christian in regard to the problem of the second coming is that of trying to understand what Christ meant. This we may never know perfectly, but we must try. Was he using vivid imagery for something that would be essentially a spiritual or inward experience? Certainly he said that the events mentioned would take place in the lifetime of persons who were alive when he spoke. "Truly, I say to you, this generation will not pass away before all these things take place" (Mark 13:30, RSV). This particular statement, because it appears in all three of the Synoptic Gospels, must have come from the written source on which all of the synoptists have drawn. Earlier Christ had said, "Truly, I say to you, there are some standing here who will not taste death before they see the kingdom of God come with power" (Mark 9:1, RSV; see Matt. 16:28 and Luke 9:27).

These important affirmations have caused many to conclude that the second coming actually occurred in the experience of Pentecost. If it did not we cannot avoid the damaging conclusion that Christ was wrong. Because I, for one, do not believe that Christ was wrong, I am driven to the interpretation that, in one sense, the second coming has already occurred and is constantly recurring when the living Christ comes into the hearts of needy and fallible men like ourselves.

What has helped me most in recent months is an application of the Christian principle of "both and" rather than "either or." It is wholly possible that Christ expected an immediate experience in human hearts and also a future event of a cataclysmic character. This hypothesis and this hypothesis alone can account for the double emphasis of Christ's own words. Why not conclude that the kingdom is both present and future and that, in both senses, it is God's doing rather than ours? I am moved when I read "The kingdom of God is in the midst of you" (RSV), especially when I realize that the crucial phrase may also be translated as "within you" (Luke 17:21, KJV). The reign of God was, in one context, affirmed rather than predicted. But, in another context, it was clearly of the future because it is obvious that much of the present course of history is a sinful revolt against the divine order. In a full sense, the kingdom has not come.

I, believe, then, that the kingdom is both present and coming. If I were to deny the future coming, I should be limiting God's power. It is wholly reasonable to believe that the ultimate solution of our manifold problems will be a mighty act of God when "the powers of the heavens shall be shaken." But, though I see that this is a reasonable inference, I also see that I should be terribly wrong to predict it at any particular time in the future, whether near or far. Christ made his rejection of such prediction explicit when he said, "But of that day or that hour no one knows, not even the angels in heaven, nor the Son, but only the Father" (Mark 13:32, RSV). It is strange that any follower of Christ, once he has seen these words, could ever engage in the prediction business. We must remember, too, the factual untrustworthiness of forecasters in the past. Over and over men have claimed to be able to read the signs of the times, but the humbling fact is that all who have announced the literal end have been proven wrong. Christ's emphasis on the irreverence of setting a date is highlighted by his saying that even he did not know.

Since the future is clearly beyond our competence to explain, the honest and humble approach is to leave all this in God's hands. If the kingdom comes fully, it will necessarily be God's doing and is therefore not our responsibility. Our task is to be watchful and as faithful as we can be today, not overconcerned about what is beyond both our power and our comprehension. In Christ's last words on earth, after the resurrection, he advocated this approach as his final earthy message. "It is not for you to know times or seasons which the Father has fixed by his own authority" (Acts 1:7, RSV). Christ ended not only by showing what is outside our competence, but also by showing what is within it. Though we cannot predict and therefore should not try to do so, we can engage in witness. "But you shall receive power when the Holy Spirit has come upon you; and you shall be my witnesses in Jerusalem and in all Judea and Samaria and to the end of the earth" (Acts 1:8, RSV).

Herein lies Christian wisdom. Our task, in connection with the second coming, is neither that of denial on the one hand nor precise dating on the other, but simple obedience to witness and to work now, doing the tasks which are within our scope. "We must," said Christ, "work the

works of him who sent me, while it is day; night comes
when no man can work" (John 9:4, RSV). We do not know
very much, but we at least know that it is still day for
you and me. The darkness will come, but it has not come
yet. God be praised.

7

Tongues

September 1972

In two former letters, those of December 1971 and of June 1972, I have done my best to deal clearly with important theological questions about which my Christian friends have been asking. These questions were those of the Jesus people and the second coming. Because the response to these letters has been generous, I am emboldened to deal with a third such issue about which some of my correspondents have already inquired. This concerns the phenomenon known as speaking with tongues.

The phenomenon in question is a very old one which has come forward with special force in the recent past. We need to understand it because it is not something which will pass away; it is far more than a passing fad. For a while the expression of vocal ecstasy was found only in Pentecostal sects; but it now appears in old, established groups, including Episcopal and Roman Catholic fellowships.

The practice we refer to is mentioned in the New Testament. What occurs is that some people, acting as part of a highly emotional fellowship, begin to speak in syllables that are incomprehensible both to themselves and to those who hear them. To the hostile listener, the syllables sound like meaningless jabber. To the friendly ones, it is thought to be meaningful, if only someone is able to interpret. In the characteristic situation, some of those present take upon themselves the task of interpretation. Often the result is ecstasy for all who are involved in the undertaking.

I am glad to say that I have been privileged to observe one form of this phenomenon. Recently, in London, while my wife and I were attending a concert of two Salvation Army bands at Regent Hall, we were surprised to hear, not far from us, a woman speaking. The Salvation Army Major who sat next to me went to her at once, attempting to calm her and thus to make it possible for the concert to proceed without interruption. I heard her say the same syllables more than once, but not one of them had any significance that I could grasp. The officer gave the woman plenty of time to express herself and then persuaded her to leave the hall.

As I meditated upon this incident I was very glad that I had encountered it. I respected the woman for her faithfulness to what she thought was her leading; but whether anyone was helped, however, was another question altogether. How much of her behavior was emotion induced by the stirring music no one can truly say.

The strangest feature of the practice in our time has been the confident conviction, on the part of some practitioners, that speaking in unknown tongues is a mark of what they call "the baptism of the Holy Spirit." Some even go so far as to claim that only those who engage in ecstatic speech are really baptized by the Spirit. The logical structure is: "If anyone is spiritually baptized, he will speak with tongues; therefore, those who do not speak with tongues are not so baptized."

That this conclusion is an arrogant one is so obvious that we are led to doubt the assumption upon which it rests. John, indeed, said that while he baptized with water, his Successor would baptize with the Holy Spirit and with fire. To hold that this necessarily leads to speaking with tongues, however, is to read something into the Scriptures which is not there.

The serious judgment of the centuries is that, while speaking with tongues is a perfectly proper development for some people, it is neither necessary nor central to the Christian faith. That there have been uncounted thousands of Christ's committed ones who have never once shared in this experience is a fact of history. God reaches men and women in so many different ways that it is always a serious error to fasten upon any particular form as essential to the total gospel. Though the experience is helpful to some, there is no probability that it will ever become universal or that it is desirable that it should become so. If it helps some people, we can simply thank God and leave the matter there.

The apostle Paul is our most trustworthy guide in this difficult matter. He was familiar with the practice already described and felt it necessary to deal with it because some of the Corinthian Christians were emphasizing it disproportionately. His method of approach was to put the matter in perspective. He showed that speaking in tongues can never be central to the gospel because it is fundamentally self-regarding. Far greater in importance, he said, is that behavior in which our primary aim is to help others rather than ourselves. The major alternative to personal ecstasy is "prophesying," which he says is of greater value.

I am helped by the way in which the crucial passage is translated in *The New English Bible:* "When a man prophesies, he is talking to men, and his words have power to build; they stimulate and they encourage. The language of ecstasy is good for the speaker himself, but it is prophesy that builds up a Christian community" (1 Cor. 14:3–4). The apostle went on to say, in the same chapter, that he, himself, was gifted in ecstatic utterance, but added, with manifest common sense, "In the congregation I would rather speak five intelligible words, for the benefit of others as well as myself, than thousands of words in the language of ecstasy" (1 Cor. 14:19, NEB). It is no wonder that this superbly gifted man, in showing that there was something else which was far superior to tongues, said, "I may speak in tongues of men or of angels, but if I am without love, I am a sounding gong or a clanging cymbal." These familiar words mean more to us when we realize that the author was referring to the phenomenon now under discussion.

Paul's point here is one of great importance in understanding the essentials of the Christian faith because religion can be almost anything, not all of it good. For instance, it is now affirmed that the use of psychedelic drugs is a religious experience, some even claiming legal protection for the practice because the First Amendment to the Constitution supports freedom of religion. All over the world there are religious establishments which do not emphasize the love of the brethren, but emphasize, instead, the comfort or elation of the communicant. Such elation may be induced by a variety of stimuli, some of which are nothing but psychological devices.

It is part of the glory of the Christian faith, at least in its characteristic manifestations, that it rejects the inadequacy of mere *feeling*. It is not enough to feel! Because we must be concerned with the needs of our brethren, basic Christianity rejects as inadequate any religion which concentrates upon inner assurance but does not lead to brotherly love as one of its fruits. This is not to say, of course, that the Christian rejects or ignores emotion, for, after all, there is a great deal of emotion in every kind of loving. The question is not whether we are emotional but whether we are emotional and no more.

Christians need to return, over and over, to Christ's own emphasis upon the love of God which leads to the love of the brother. If we feel good in the process, there is nothing wrong with that; but the warm glow is fundamentally a by-product rather than an end to be sought. The Christian does not try to become happy; he operates as an instrument of the divine will and lets the consequences take care of themselves. The only way to get happiness is to forget it! We must not seek to induce inner states, making these our primary aim. The true Christian is not one who goes about taking his spiritual pulse in order to know how he is progressing in his pilgrimage. His first task is to try to learn, if he can, what God's will for him is and then to do it. The consequences are in God's hands, never in his own.

What is encouraging about the emergence of the tongues in our generation is that it is at least an evidence of vitality. The movement, though beset with dangers and pitfalls, is, in any case, a welcome contrast to religious dullness. One of the chief reasons why it has caught on so widely in denominations of undoubted respectability is that people are dissatisfied with the kind of religious experience in which nothing occurs. They are tired of going through a ritual in which there are no new decisions and therefore no changed lives. When people begin to shout, that may not be the best thing for them to do; but it is better than doing nothing. As Yokefellows we welcome vitality, but we are especially eager that the vitality exhibit itself in a pattern of wholeness rather than in one in which people are encouraged to be satisfied with merely a fragment of the gospel.

8

Healing

December 1972

The current interest in Christian healing is widespread. After years of neglect, the idea that healing is possible or even normal has appeared all across the entire Christian spectrum. Expectations which were once limited to Christian Scientists and a few other groups are now shared by many different denominations, among which the Episcopal Church is most prominent.

The revival of belief in healing has come, in part, as the natural result of careful attention to the New Testament record. Almost anyone who reads the Gospels with any care is bound to observe that healing, far from being tangential, was an essential element in the original Christian revolution. Not only did Christ, in his earthly life, engage in the healing of a variety of diseases; he also expected his followers to engage in a similar practice. Over and over we learn that he sent out his disciples, not merely to preach and to teach, but also to heal both bodies and spirits. Particularly, it was expected that those who were Christ's emissaries would cast out demons. Crucial to the entire gospel are the following admonitions: "Preach as you go, saying, 'The kingdom of heaven is at hand.' Heal the sick, raise the dead, cleanse lepers, cast out demons" (Matt. 10:7–8, RSV).

To the casual outsider, the early Christian phenomenon must have seemed more of a healing movement than anything else. Certainly it did not seem like a new religion, for there was no ritual and no priestly class. Indeed, the chief participants were what we should call laymen. The most obvious feature of the movement consisted of the fact that there was the emergence of a new order in which people became whole (i.e., well). When two of the disciples of John came to Jesus to ask whether he were really the expected One, he limited his answer, for the most part, to the healing effects of what was transpiring. "Go," said Christ, "and shew John again those things which ye do hear and see: the blind receive their sight, and the lame walk, the lepers are cleansed, and the deaf hear, the dead are raised up, and the poor have the gospel preached to them" (Matt. 11:4–5). It is not unimportant to note that the emphasis upon healing precedes that on preaching.

A great part of the work of the early Christian community was in the field of what we call mental illness. In the passage from the earliest Gospel which may reasonably be considered the first account of the emerging church, in contrast to both the Temple and the synagogue, Christ, we are told, called unto him the twelve and began to send them forth "and gave them power over unclean spirits" (Mark 6:7). We naturally expect more in his directions to them, but this is all. There is not a word about giving sermons! The result of this first public venture is simply stated as follows: "And they cast out many devils and anointed with oil many that were sick, and healed them" (Mark 6:13).

The widespread loss of an emphasis so clear is difficult to understand, but of the loss there is no doubt. During the recent past there have been entire segments of the

Christian community in which healing has not been the normal expectation at all. The church has tended to stress many features while minimizing the one feature which Christ stressed most. There are, of course, several concurrent reasons for this; but one of the most influential of them has been our growing conviction of the cultural necessity of a sharp division of labor. The growth of professions has had much to do with this tendency. Thus, with the development of legal competence, it has seemed natural to leave the law to lawyers without interference from the rest of us. In similar fashion, it has seemed reasonable to leave the entire area of disease and health to the physicians who are supposed to be competent in such matters. What then is left to the representatives of Christ? That is extremely hard to say. The general assumption seems to be that all that remains is something vaguely called religion. In the nature of the case the field that is left is constantly decreasing in area. The mortician takes over death; the teacher takes over education; the psychologist takes over counseling. What remains?

Another important reason for the long decline of Christian healing is philosophical. A form of naturalism is widely accepted without examination and consequently without serious criticism. This does not follow necessarily from science, though many people think that it does. The central conviction is that all events are determined by natural laws. People with particular germs contract particular diseases, and that is the end of the matter. If the germs are scientifically removed, the people get well; and if not, they do not get well. In essence, this is simply a dogmatic rejection of any supernatural view of reality. The strangest feature of this philosophy is that so many accept it uncritically, not even recognizing that they are being dogmatic.

What is required of Christians is a philosophy of sufficient magnitude to liberate people from both a strict division of labor and a naturalistic metaphysic. Most of us, being grateful for modern medicine, count physicians among our closest associates. But this need not make us draw the conclusion that health is the proprietary domain of doctors. Every honest doctor is keenly aware of his own limitations in a fashion which his patients often are not. Every doctor knows that he cannot heal; all that he can do is to help to remove some of the barriers to healing. There is no necessity to choose between prayer and the use of the doctor's skill because this is one of the situations in which *and* is obviously more intelligent than *or*.

The rejection of naturalism is intrinsic to the Christian faith. Insofar as we are loyal to Christ we are convinced that, with God, all things are possible (Mark 10:27). Natural law, far from being sovereign, is subservient to God's purpose. A strict naturalism, which denies the objective power of prayer to produce events, is simply a repudiation of the gospel of Christ. The Christian operates in a world of greater magnitude than does the dogmatist who claims, in his arrogance, that there are things that God cannot do. Natural laws, we believe, are God's vehicles rather than his controllers.

There is a tendency to suppose that, while miraculous restoration of health occurred during Christ's earthly life, it is not to be expected now because we are in a different dispensation. By this device people are able to defend their contemporary lack of belief in healing. The crucial error of this kind of thinking is that it operates upon the false assumption that Christ is dead, whereas the heart of all basic Christianity is that Christ is alive and that he is just as available to his followers now as he was when he first sent his disciples forth to heal. If we take the resurrection seriously, we do not believe that Christ's power to heal was ended with the crucifixion. In short, the operation is meant to be continuous; and we, unworthy as we are, are expected to be his healing instruments. Every Christian ought, therefore, to be engaged in the healing ministry in the living present.

Though the contemporary recovery of the healing idea has been a remarkable asset in our generation and is basically sound, it has also been beset with dangers. The potential gain has been marred by the fact that some have set themselves up as professional healers with an atmosphere of showmanship. In some instances there has been actual trickery with a consequent loss of credibility. In some public meetings, advertised as healing services, there appear to be signals from scouts in the congregation, enabling the leader to know, before the individual appears, what the nature of his trouble is. Whenever healing becomes a racket, the consequent harm is terrible because it takes advantage of people's hopes and sorrows for the personal gain of the operator. Some of the books on healing, unfortunately, claim too much and are too simplistic. They are always too simplistic when they fail to point out that there is no healing technique that always succeeds.

The thoughtful Christian stands here, as he does in so many other situations, in the middle. He must reject the simplifications of both the right and the left. He must resist equally the dogmatism of the person who says that divine healing cannot occur and the dogmatism of the person who says it always occurs, providing the conditions are met. The Christian has to be a realist; and, as a realist, he knows that our fondest hopes are sometimes denied us, even when our prayers have been both sincere and persistent. Death finally comes to all, including the most tender and devout. There is no simple formula by means of which we always get what we ask. Whatever else the power of prayer may be, we can at least be sure that it does not work mechanically.

In regard to healing, the honest Christian must always be aware of dual dangers. It is equally erroneous to deny the possibility of healing and to take pride in performing it as though the power is our own. Our safety lies in the genuine humility which makes us realize that, at best, we are only instrumental. Our prayer may be "O God, make me an instrument of thy healing." By such a spirit we are liberated from the temptation to suppose that we are more than we are. In reality, our ignorance is very great; and certainly we cannot know very much of what God's will is. This is why the stated or unstated feature of every Christian prayer is "Not my will but thine be done."

Because God is like Christ, we have good reason to believe that he wills our health. Christ came that we might live abundantly, rather than in some meager fashion. Our first task is to try to eliminate from our lives and from the lives of others any barriers to the fullness of health and vitality to which we are called.

9

Astrology

March 1973

The topic of astrology is one which is both prominent and puzzling. As a visit to almost any bookstore can verify, there has been, in our generation, something like an occult explosion. Books on astrology, witchcraft, demonology, and related themes are numerous, and they are numerous because there is a strong demand among potential readers. Many daily newspapers include astrological forecasts, regular sections being devoted to the use of the zodiac in fortune telling. If there were not a widespread demand, valuable space would not be employed in this fashion.

The belief that we are in a new age, the "Age of Aquarius," is supported by many references, both on Broadway and in titles of contemporary books. Constant repetition has led great numbers to accept astrological ideas uncritically.

The problem of astrology is particularly difficult for committed Christians because, on the one hand, Christians tend to welcome any kind of spiritual interest, while, on the other hand, they honor the biblical heritage which rejects the occult at all levels. If Christians do not think carefully, they are almost sure to find themselves in an untenable position. Here is one of the points at which we must seek to help one another.

During the past year in one American city, a high school teacher of French, having placed on the blackboard in front of her students a full diagram of the zodiac with all of the major signs, asked each of the class members to say under what sign he or she had been born. All responded with the exception of one sixteen-year-old boy. Finally the teacher addressed the boy individually, asking, "Which of these is your sign, John?" "Not any of them," replied the boy. "I am under the sign of the cross." Not another word was said on the subject; and, at the beginning of the next session, the board was clean.

The reason why this particular boy was able to make a courageous and unpopular witness was that he knew something of the message of the Bible. He knew, for instance, that the claims of astrology are repudiated by the biblical writers with remarkable consistency, the incompetence of the astrologers being mentioned four times in the book of Daniel. The greatest of the prophets sought to set men free from all superstitious practices and to center on the living God instead. Magic, sorcery, and star gazing were classified together as enemies of theistic faith. "Let now the astrologers, the stargazers, the monthly prognosticators, stand up, and save thee" (Isa. 47:13).

Astrology appeared very early in civilization as a precursor of astronomy. Both astronomy and astrology deal with stars, but the former is a positive science while the latter is not. Because one of the early centers of astrology was Babylon, it was during the exile that the Israelites first came into direct contact with occult practices and claims. Thus, in Daniel, Chaldeans and astrologers are practically synonymous terms. The basic premise of the entire operation was the conviction that the motion of the stars had direct influence upon human events and the development of human character. It was not really difficult to observe the orderly movements of the heavenly bodies, this orderliness providing the soothsayers with an appearance of credibility.

The deepest motivation for practices of divination, in either the ancient or the modern world, is the desire of the human heart to learn the future. If only we could know, the ordinary reasoning goes, we should be better able to adjust to what is coming. The desire for this knowledge is so great that shady practices, no matter how illicit, always find some acceptance. Herein lies the pathos of the present situation. Though we boast about our educational advances, people appear to be as gullible as ever. It is at this point that the biblical faith can join with genuine science in saving people from disappointment so far as they are willing to listen. We can thank God for the tough-mindedness of our basic Christian faith, which recognizes that the chief threat to the kingdom of Christ lies not in outright materialism but in a false spiritualism, such as that represented by soothsayers.

It is fortunate that, in the development of Christianity, we have had a powerful and continuous emphasis upon truth. It is not enough, we believe, to have a faith; it must be a faith which is verifiable. No matter how comforting it may be, if a faith is not true, it is evil. Judged by this test, the occult is a miserable failure. The reason why astrology is not a science and has no standing at all in the scientific community is that it does not deal with what is objectively true. It does not produce evidence of the kind which could make it a reputable science comparable to chemistry, biology, or astronomy. There is no accumulated body of knowledge to support the conviction that the positions of the constellations have any effect on the destiny of human beings, either individually or in groups.

There is a slight appearance of scientific validity in astrological forecasting in reference to the precession of the equinoxes, which leads to a revolution of the celestial sphere each 26,000 years. But there is no rational basis for supposing that this slow change has any effect whatever upon the events of human life. It does not even have an effect on the seasons. The best cure for addiction to astrology is a good course in astronomy, but this is what the upholders of the cult will not undertake. In fact, many of the adherents openly reject the scientific mentality as something from which they are liberated when they enter the new age.

Fortunately, the biblical rejection of astrology does not stand alone. The tough-mindedness of William Shakespeare is gratefully remembered in this connection. One of his best-known sentences in *Julius Caesar* is: "The fault, dear Brutus, is not in our stars,/But in ourselves, that we are underlings."

In *King Lear* the recognition that the claims of astrology are false is even more definite:

"This is the excellent foppery of the world, that, when we are sick in fortune,—often surfeit of our own behaviour,—we make guilty of our disasters the sun, the moon, and the stars: as if we were villains by necessity; fools by heavenly compulsion; knaves, thieves, and treachers by special predominance; drunkards, liars, and adulterers by an enforced obedience of planetary influence."

The saddest feature of the new cult is the revelation which it provides of the spiritual emptiness of many lives. Having no sound basis of faith, millions are turning to substitutes. Knowing nothing of the Bible, they take seriously the inane remarks of some hack writer in the daily newspaper who writes, "Important decisions may be made in your life today." Here is vivid verification of the truth of Christ's observation that the house of the spirit cannot remain empty (Matt. 12:44). In the long run, the only alternative to a noble faith is an ignoble one; the maintenance of a spiritual vacuum is really an impossibility!

The committed Christian must see the growth of occult practices as both a challenge and an opportunity. The pathetic demonstrations of spiritual hunger will not, if we understand our own position, delude us into even a quasi-acceptance of anti-Christian cults. It will, instead, increase our determination to provide our brothers everywhere with a sound alternative. But the first step is to be clear.

10

Weakness and Strength

June 1973

Questions are sometimes more revealing than are answers. To help people ask the right questions is an important part of our ministry because, once the problem is clarified, we are already on the way to a solution.

The most insistent question which the actual and potential readers of this letter seem now to be asking refers to the endurance of the church. Is the church of Christ, some now ask, approaching its demise? Perhaps, they say, after generations of existence, the church is now at the end of its tether and will soon cease to be. This suggestion is seriously put forth not only by those who are consciously outside the church or antagonistic to it but also by those who are devoted members and supporters.

The best way to approach this question is to face whatever bad news there is without minimizing any of it. In the first place, we must consider the statistical reports. For the first time in many years the record of growth has been reversed. Far from keeping up with the increase in population the major denominations, particularly the Methodists and Presbyterians, report actual numerical decline. The most striking drop is in Sunday School participation. In the overall gloomy picture there is no significant difference between Protestants and Roman Catholics.

One of the most revealing evidences of decline is the difficulty experienced in securing recruits for full-time religious vocations. So difficult is it to enroll young men as students for the priesthood that one of the largest of the Roman Catholic seminaries has closed one entire building. The orders of sisters have so few applicants that some are only one-third as large as they were ten years ago. One consequence of this decline is the extreme difficulty of providing parochial schools with teachers. When secular teachers are hired and paid the going wage, the expense of maintaining schools is sometimes raised to a point at which continued existence is impossible.

The Protestant theological seminaries are having, to a somewhat lesser degree, the same problems which are encountered by their Catholic counterparts. One of the most prestigious has about half as many students as were enrolled ten years ago. In the major denominations there are still enough pastors to fill the required places, but many of these persons are both restive and discouraged. Seldom today do the ablest young men elect to the pastorate when they graduate from college. The keenest young men tend to choose work with computers or to enter either medicine or law. The contrast between the mood of the law and medical schools, on the one hand, and the theological schools, on the other, is very depressing. The law schools especially have no problems of morale, partly because they have no problems of enrollment.

On all sides is the evidence of lack of youth in the church. The fact that most strong congregations employ youth ministers does not seem to make much difference. Only the very young are attracted to the usual programs, and these tend to drop out in late adolescence. Sometimes they come back in maturity, particularly when they have children of their own; but the resulting age gap is really frightening.

Once we were able to take comfort in the fact that, though our college-age young people were not visible in the home congregation, they were being reached in the colleges they attended. Though this was once largely true it is not, for the most part, true now. Student–Christian institutions, such as the Wesley Foundation, now tend, on the whole, to be ineffective. The part they play in campus life is, in most places, negligible. Even the Christian colleges give very little reason for hope. Most of them have abandoned the practice of required chapel attendance on the supposition that voluntary attendance will take the place of it; but the disappointment in this connection is almost total. With the prospect of poor attendance, the best speakers are not usually willing to participate in a dying effort.

Some of the lay movements that once engendered hope have now declined conspicuously. Presbyterian Men, for example, constituted a really powerful movement twenty years ago; but now it is relatively insignificant. A similar decline has appeared in Christian journalism. Some journals have merged, not in strength but in weakness. The *Christian Century,* once so influential, is barely able to keep going. And several denominational magazines survive only because they are heavily subsidized.

When we put all of these gloomy facts together, as we must if we are honest, the resulting picture is certainly a dark one. If the committed Christian is to find any ground of hope, he will certainly have to go beyond superficial evidences.

My chief purpose in writing this particular letter to my reading friends is to provide them with that combination of realism and hope which the gospel requires. To fail to face the discouraging facts is a denial of the gospel, but a failure to probe deeply enough to other aspects is equally disloyal. The encouraging facts are such that they are not likely to be recorded in the newspapers or on television. Three signs of hope I shall mention now.

The first sign of hope I see is that people respond strongly today when they have reason to think they will encounter genuine vitality. While they lose interest in the routine of the mainline congregation, they respond with dynamism at other points. Our recent Annual Yokefellow Conference on March 23–24, 1973, is one vivid demonstration of this fact. The desire to attend was almost overwhelming. More than two hundred applicants had to be turned away from the opening session because there was simply not sufficient room for them to sit at the tables. As it was, the Earlham Dining Room accommodated more people than it has ever done previously. The spirit was infectious. As I looked at the faces of the men and women from many states, I realized that I was looking at the church and that it is far from dead. In one financial offering, made on Saturday afternoon, the men who counted the money were amazed to find a total of $2,515. There was no problem of giving when committed people saw a reason. The lay conference at Lake Barkley, Kentucky, prior to the Annual Yokefellow Conference, had a similar problem with more applicants than places. It is the kind of problem we like to face. That it can occur shows that the total pessimism so often expressed today is unjustified.

A second sign of hope is the recognition that the supposed decline of congregations is far from universal. To the surprise of many observers, some of the conservative groups are booming, while the prestigious congregations become smaller. While the more liberal fellowships are dying, the more evangelical ones are growing. There are many reasons for this development, but the most important reason seems to be that people are unified by positive beliefs rather than by their doubts. Whenever the church becomes a mere ethical culture society or concentrates only on political and economic issues, it declines. But when people are helped to believe something profound about their relationship to the living God, power is almost sure to emerge.

A third sign of hope lies in the development of new adult education. Though the Sunday School movement has seemed to decline, serious adult study of theology is booming where it is seriously tried. For example, in St. Paul's Church, Richmond, Virginia, the rector now teaches a class in theology from ten to eleven on Sunday morning, the class averaging more than two hundred in attendance. The people respond when they have reason to believe that they will be introduced to matters of real importance in their lives. At Sun City Center, Florida, the church is introducing the idea of welcoming for several consecutive weeks a "theologian in residence." The people respond to the kind of teaching which they would have welcomed in college but were not given. If this can succeed in one place, it can succeed in others.

My best advice is to avoid hasty conclusions. The church of Jesus Christ has faced hard times before and has survived. New life tends to emerge when we least expect it. In any case, we do not expect easy lives. To know that we were made for what is arduous is to know something of enduring significance. The balanced truth is never that of either complacency or despair but the recognition that a wide door is open, and there are many adversaries (1 Cor. 16:9).

11

Autobiography

December 1973

The experiences of the last few months have been revealing ones to me. My most demanding experience has been
the writing of my autobiography, which I finally decided
to entitle *While It Is Day*. The phrase, as you may know,
comes from John 9:4. It represents, in part, my strong
conviction about the importance of time, a conviction
which all Yokefellows share when they seek to practice
the discipline of time. No day is long enough, and every
human life is pitifully short. The amazing fact for you
and me is that we are still privileged to live. My gratitude
is unlimited.

What has been revealing is the experience of looking
at my entire life in retrospect. The memories of those to
whom I am indebted rise up to move me deeply. Many
of them have already moved to a better country, but this
does not dim the reality of their contribution to my life.
They have left markers along the road to tell me where
some of the dangers are and also to tell me where true
joys are to be found.

What has been most moving to me in looking at my
life from the perspective of the present is the consideration
of the various forks in the road. Each reader of this letter
who has stood and has looked down more than one possible

road will understand. One big decision in my own life came soon after graduation from Harvard Divinity School, when I was forced to decide whether to enter the pastoral ministry or the ministry of college teaching. The fact that the decision was made nearly forty-seven years ago does not diminish its vividness in the least.

In a profound sense each person is the sum of his decisions, and each one is important because each leads to many others. Humans are, among other things, decision makers. And herein lies much of the anguish as well as the glory of being human. Often we make decisions which we have reason to regret.

One of the major turning points of my life came in connection with a passage of Scripture which became very important to me about the time of my departure from Stanford University for Earlham College. The idea of a new order was seething in my mind, though there was as yet no thought of employing the biblical reference to the yoke of Christ. That did not come until May 1949. But before Christ's invitation to wear his yoke struck me forcefully, I had already begun to realize that power lies in a Christ-centered faith.

When I preached my last sermon as Chaplain of Stanford University in December 1945, already realizing that I was an evangelical Christian, I selected as my text Romans 1:16, "For I am not ashamed of the gospel: it is the power of God for salvation to every one who has faith" (RSV). This was the basis of my Christmas sermon twenty-eight years ago. I saw that the only true way to celebrate Christmas is to center our minds on Christ himself rather than on any of the fringes of the faith. I saw also that the validation of the faith lies in its consequences, the chief of which are the changed lives of those who are turned by their own confrontation with Christ from weakness to strength. I saw, finally, that an apologetic or tentative faith is worth nothing at all. I did not see where this would lead me and my companions, but I recognized clearly that in commitment to Jesus Christ there is a genuine alternative to the meaninglessness with which thousands of lives are burdened. At the greatest single turning point of my life I determined that my faith must be not only rational but also Christ-centered. Consequently, I embarked on a course on which I have remained ever since.

The contemplation of my life in its totality has also led me to understand better the steps by which the Yokefellow idea has emerged in our generation. Indeed, one of the eight chapters of the autobiography is devoted entirely to the growth of my mind on this idea which you and I now share. At first, neither I nor anyone else saw more than a fraction of what it means to Christians to be yoked. New developments now appear with astonishing variety, and we wonder why we did not see them earlier. For example, I have just returned from a mission in North Carolina and I return full of amazement. Not only did I dedicate a new Yokefellow Retreat Center; I also visited one of seven Yoke Service Centers which are demonstrating the outward as well as the inward journey of the committed Christian. I had visited the Yoke Center at Forest City nearly six years ago, but I was not really aware of its subsequent growth. Located in a business area, where people can reach it easily, this center specializes in yoking together the needs of people with the skills of those able to help. Contact is quickly made with experts in healing, in education, and in finance because a list of helpers is kept up to date. Consequently, no person is turned away. Moreover, the church members, regardless of denomination, have contributed used clothing and other supplies in quantity. There is a small library for the use of those who have time to sit and think. The ox-yoke on the wall provides all visitors with a reminder of Christ's call.

Once we had no work like that at Forest City. But now, in addition to the seven centers which bear our name, there are ten others without this specific wording but all encouraged by Yokefellows. In every case the key to the redemptive operation is the conviction that we must link worship and work, inner life and outer service, prayer and tough thinking. Each of these is inadequate alone but is powerful in conjunction with another aspect of the gospel. The Yoke Service Center is a breakthrough comparable to that of the Prison Ministry when it began.

The yoke of Christ is the symbol of the conjunct life. Throughout the New Testament is a phrase which is a binding and penetrating thread, the phrase "one another." In one small book, 1 Thessalonians, probably the first New Testament book that was written, this particular phrase appears five times. Nearly all of the most precious book in our lives is about the fellowship. Even when Christ sent out his ambassadors, he did not send them out one by one but two by two. After the sad encounter at the synagogue at Nazareth, when the new Christian strategy really began, the teams commissioned were yoked teams. Christ called the twelve "and began to send them out two by two, and gave them authority over the unclean spirits" (Mark 6:7, RSV). Thus even the work of healing was a team affair. There have been single yokes in some parts of the world, but the yoke of Christ is always the double yoke.

12

Macedonia

June 1974

This letter is being written in a setting which moves me deeply. I am in the Macedonian city of Thessalonica, highly conscious of certain events which transpired here 1,924 years ago when the apostle Paul and his brave team of Christians arrived here after their harsh experience at Philippi. I am stirred by the recognition that I am in the very city in which the first words of the New Testament were heard as they were read aloud. I refer to 1 Thessalonians, generally recognized as the first contribution to the greatest book of the world. As I try to reconstruct in my mind the ancient scene, I am almost overwhelmed with wonder.

My greatest sense of wonder involves the stupendous fact that the little fellowship formed here so long ago actually survived! The dangers, both external and internal, were both numerous and immense. We must remember that the vast majority of the people had never heard of Christ at all and also that the local Jews, who might have been expected to be friendly, were violently antagonistic to the new message. The few persons whom Paul gathered lacked both money and prestige. They had neither buildings nor ecclesiastical structure to hold them together, and there were no established traditions to guide them. By

ordinary human standards the strange new movement was
almost certain to come to an end after a brief period of
enthusiasm. After all, as Gamaliel sagely observed, the phenomenon of temporary loyalty had already occurred many
times before (Acts 5:36–37). What reason did any observer
have to suppose that the novelty would not likewise wear
off at Thessalonica?

One reason for survival was the effectiveness of the written word. Nobody, of course, had the slightest idea that
the New Testament was being originated, though this is
what actually occurred. As Paul left Macedonia, to which
he had been drawn so dramatically while he was in Troy,
he departed with a haunting sense of concern for the little
fellowship on which so much of the future depended. As
he traveled southward, his worry grew. What if they
should bicker among themselves? What if they should so
interpret Christ's coming again that they would cease to
work? What if they would stop praying? So great was
Paul's concern that, soon after the arrival of the Christian
team in Athens, he dispatched his trusted deputy, Timothy, sending him back to the very town where I now sit,
in order to check on the development. Sending Timothy
back north at a time when he was obviously needed in
the south is a vivid indication of how worried Paul was
and how deeply he cared.

After Paul had arrived in Corinth for his long stay of
eighteen months, Timothy came back and reported on his
second visit to Macedonia. This report led to the writing
of Paul's letter, which eventually became the first book
of the amazing compilation on which so many millions
of persons still depend. Paul could not possibly realize,
as he wrote, that he was producing something of genuine
magnitude. Actually 1 Thessalonians is the beginning of

Christian literature, a literature which now includes count-
less volumes. Every river, in addition to numerous tribu-
taries, has some genuine beginning without which the entire stream would not be. The tiny letter which we so
prize occupies this position in the stream of Christian
literature.

The letter was sent, and the little company listened as
it was read aloud. Their commitment was accordingly
strengthened, and this became one of the chief reasons
for their continuance in spite of so many reasons for discouragement. The key expression of the first book of Christian literature was "one another," an expression which
appears five times. Here, Paul reminded them, was their
secret weapon against the threat of extinction. The climac-
tic sentence is "Therefore encourage one another and build
one another up, just as you are doing" (1 Thess. 5:11, RSV).
Christians were strong because they supported one another. As the key verse indicates, such mutual support
was not a mere dream but something which occurred in
fact. Among the amazing early Christians there were many
forms of ministry, but the ministry of encouragement was
paramount.

Once the literary pattern had been established, the apostle went on to write many other letters, each addressed
to one of the fragile fellowships about which he cared so
greatly and on which so much of the future of the church
depended. Not one of these fellowships owned a building
in which to meet, but that constituted no serious problem.
They had one another; they were in direct communion
with the one to whom they were committed; and they
had the priceless treasure of the written word. Without
this word the Christian movement would either have disap-
peared or become so altered as to have little resemblance

to the original pattern. Today, as Christians, we make many mistakes; but we have always the incalculable advantage of checking the pattern by the standard of the Word.

All Christian scholars now recognize that the epistles were produced earlier than were the Gospels. If the New Testament were printed in the order of writing, the first book would, accordingly, be 1 Thessalonians rather than Matthew. Once the early letters had been written, there was an instant demand for more precise knowledge of how Christ lived, taught, died, and rose. The gospels were thus produced in response to a felt need. Finally, all the separate books which we now bind into one volume were completed. And, accordingly, something of intrinsic value was added to the human story. In this volume we have a record, not of speculation but of astounding events. A redemptive fellowship actually spread miraculously through the Hellenic world and then survived. Fortunately, we can read the astounding story in the book called Acts. The double book, which is rightly described as "Luke-Acts," all by the same author, is of supreme worth. To none are we more grateful than to Luke, to whom we owe our chief knowledge of what occurred in the key area where I now sit.

I feel not only grateful to Luke, but very close to him here in Thessalonica. He and I are both Gentiles, and we both are related to Christ's resurrection by looking at the evidence. We are on the same side of the historical divide. Some scholars believe that Luke was originally from Macedonia and that Luke's familiarity with the region was one of the factors in Paul's decision to come here. In any case, Luke involved himself in the narrative, writing, "Setting sail therefore from Troas, we made a direct voyage to Samothrace, and the following day Neapo-

lis, and from there to Philippi" (Acts 16:11–12, RSV). It
moves me to know, as I write, that I shall be at both Neapo-
lis and Philippi tomorrow.

Certain ideas that have been in my mind for a long
time are brought together in this place with great vividness. The wonder of our history is precious, but it is of
little value if we are historians and no more. Our concen-
tration of thought now must be upon the reenactment
of the miracle. The early fellowship survived and flour-
ished, not because of a single causal factor but by virtue
of a unique combination. The early Christians of Greece
were imperfect people, much as we are; but they combined
a belief, a commitment, and a fellowship. If any one of
the three was omitted, failure was bound to ensue. They
believed that Jesus was truly the image of the invisible
Father and that he was alive; they were committed to him
and to his cause; they were yoked with one another as a
consequence of being yoked with him.

As I go on to Philippi, I am keenly aware that it was
in the letter to the Christian group in this ancient city
that Paul employed the magnificent term *Yokefellow* as a
synonym for a practicing follower of Christ. I feel very
fortunate in my experiences this time in Greece because
I have been able to stand where great things have been
done and said. As a part of the "Adventure in Living,"
it is my assignment to speak to my 135 associates in five
significant places—the Acropolis in Athens, the Tribune
in Corinth, the Rotunda of Thessalonica, the scene of the
first Christian gathering of the Philippians, and Ephesus.
My overwhelming conviction is that if the people could
become new persons 1,924 years ago, we can do the same
in our time.

13

The Bible

September 1974

For several weeks it has been increasingly clear to me that I should devote the whole of one letter to the Christian understanding of the Bible. The more I move about the country the more I see the need of this approach. Many say openly that they seek guidance on this important subject.

If the Christian faith is to survive, the place to begin is the necessity of the Bible. Apart from the written record, Christian practice would have become so diverse that its different expressions would have had almost nothing in common. But once the New Testament had come into existence, there was a standard of reference in terms of which all variants could be judged. It is, therefore, something for which our gratitude is boundless. If it were not for the Book, we should not even be.

We understand the New Testament better when we realize that, in an important sense, its production was unintentional. The early Christians of Hebrew origin were familiar, of course, with what we call the Old Testament, which they often quoted. Christ himself quoted the Hebrew Scriptures, particularly Deuteronomy, Psalms, and Isaiah. Many of the early Christian sermons employed texts found in the Hebrew Scriptures and saw their own messages as fulfillment. The Greek Christians, by contrast, had no experience of this kind and were not even familiar with the idea of sacred Scripture. Neither Jewish nor Greek Christians had, in the beginning, any idea of a new volume of sacred writings.

The New Testament arose, bit by bit, as a conscious effort to meet human need. The first of these small writings were produced about the middle of the first century A.D., the earliest being letters written by the apostle Paul to encourage the feeble little bands which had emerged in the Greek world. If Paul had been told that he was producing something both permanent and universal he would have been the most surprised man in the world; yet that turned out to be the case. The earliest writers sought to meet a temporary need, but in the end they did far more than this. They wrote deathless words which can give both guidance and strength to men and women living now in scattered areas more than nineteen hundred years later.

The New Testament may be rightly seen as the greatest book of the world. Valuable in itself, it is even more valuable when combined with the Old Testament, which provides so much background for its ideas.

No body of literature has been the subject of more intense scholarly study than has the New Testament. One consequence is that we are able to reach reliable conclusions about the order in which the separate books were written and can see evidence of development. For example, it is now obvious that the Gospels were composed, in their present form, after the writing of the small letters addressed to individual congregations.

The letters were, for the most part, addressed not to Greeks in general but to localized fellowships experiencing particular problems. The Gospels came about as a result of widespread demand, particularly on the part of Greek Christians, for a fuller understanding of what Christ did and said. What we call the Synoptic Gospels, Mark, Matthew, and Luke, were produced much earlier than was the Fourth Gospel, which takes a different approach to the story. The evidence indicates that this, the best loved of all the books of the New Testament collection, was written at Ephesus about A.D. 100. The apostle John was nearly one hundred years old and was able to emphasize not merely what Jesus said but what he meant. Christ had said, "I have yet many things to say to you, but you cannot bear them now" (John 16:12, RSV); and the fact that some of these appeared in the Fourth Gospel helps to explain the radical way in which it differs from the Synoptics.

It has been part of my good fortune in my long life to know personally some of the scholarly men who have translated the Scriptures in our generation. Thus I have valued the friendship of Henry J. Cadbury, one of the chief producers of the Revised Standard Version, and have had some acquaintance with both William Barclay of Scotland and J. B. Phillips of England. I have been impressed by the way in which the wonder of the entire biblical phenomenon has grown in the minds of such scholars. The more they study, the more amazing the story becomes in their estimation. It must have been God's doing—for with men the total product was not even intended. Over and over I turn to the words of Dr. Phillips:

> As the years have passed . . . my conviction has grown that the New Testament is in a quite special sense inspired. It is not magical, nor is it faultless: human beings wrote it. But by something which I would not hesitate to describe as a miracle, there is a concentration upon that area of inner truth

which is fundamental and ageless. That, I believe, is the reason why millions of people have heard the voice of God speaking to them through these seemingly artless pages.

What I want most to say to my friends who read this letter, now numbering about four thousand persons, is that it is possible, in approaching the Bible, to combine both reverence and intellectual integrity. The wonder is increased rather than decreased by honest study. In my own experience this has gone on for more than fifty years. I have been delighted to discover that difficult problems actually yield to further study. For example, many are puzzled today by the words in the fourteenth chapter of 1 Corinthians, about the place of women in the Christian faith. The words of Paul seem harsh, particularly when he says of Christian women, "If there is anything they desire to know, let them ask their husbands at home. For it is shameful for a woman to speak in church" (1 Cor. 14:35, RSV). What study reveals, however, is that this is not the apostle's last word on this important subject. There is good reason to conclude that Galatians was produced later than 1 Corinthians, and in this book we find evidence of a striking development: "There is neither Jew nor Greek, there is neither slave nor free, there is neither male nor female; for you are all one in Christ" (Gal.3:28, RSV). Here is a conclusion of undoubted grandeur which means that the Christian experience is one which utterly transcends sexual differences, just as it transcends differences of race. Part of the wonder of the biblical message is the wonder of growth. But we could not understand this apart from the meticulous work in which so many have been engaged for more than a century.

I hope that all who read this quarterly letter will learn more and more by direct experience how great a spiritual resource the Bible is. It is in no sense obsolete, for there has been no alteration either in the character of God or in the essentials of human need. Such a classic as Psalm 139 is exactly as applicable to our contemporary problems as it was when produced centuries before the Christian era. Personally, I have been helped by the words of the scholars who worked for years to give us the Revised Standard Version of the entire Bible two decades ago. They said in conclusion:

> The Bible is more than a historical document to be preserved. And it is more than a classic of English literature to be cherished and admired. It is a record of God's dealing with men, of God's revelation of himself and his will. It records the life and work of him in whom the Word of God became flesh and dwelt among men.

Christ is the Word who "became flesh and dwelt among us." Our faith is not in language but in a Person. Yet we are grateful for the language because, without it, we could not know him to whom it points.

14

Conditions of Vitality

December 1974

During the year which is now ending, I have partici-
pated in a good many interviews with representatives of
newspapers as well as radio and television stations. In these
I am nearly always asked what I think the present religious
situation is. "Is religion declining or flourishing?"

In answering such a question I am compelled, in honesty,
to show that the word *religion* is ambiguous. Because it
may mean almost anything, from that which is grossly
superstitious to that which is highly rational, I cannot
make an intelligent answer unless the reference is made
more precise. I find it helpful to point out that, while I
am not much interested in what is vaguely called religion,
I am vitally interested in the cause of Jesus Christ.

Even after the question has been sharpened and made
to refer specifically to the Christian faith, it is not possible
to give a simple answer because the situation is complex.
In honesty, the person being interviewed is forced to reply
that some Christian efforts are failing while others are
demonstrating marked vitality. Since there is both darkness and light, we dare not affirm one of these without
mentioning the other. The Christian who understands the
gospel, while never denying the existence of darkness, sees
that "The light continues to shine in the darkness and

the darkness has never extinguished it" (John 1:5, *The New Testament* 1, *Gospels and Acts of the Apostles*). We owe to William Barclay this very helpful translation of an important passage of Scripture.

In this particular letter it is not necessary for me to dwell on the discouraging features of the current scene because we all know what they are. There are reduced budgets for the World Christian Mission, and there is reduced attendance at many Christian gatherings. This is one side of the story, but there is another side which is not widely known; and it is this side which needs to be presented at this Christmas season of 1974. The surprising news is that some churches are today exceedingly strong! Just recently I have visited a few congregations which give me renewed hope, and I trust that knowledge of them will give hope to others who read this letter.

It will help us in our own efforts if we can learn what it is that makes a few churches strong when so many others are lamentably weak. We need to try to ascertain where the power is and why it is exhibited in some situations rather than others. What are the chief conditions of vitality? As I observe the Christian scene, I conclude that the chief secrets of spiritual power are four, as follows:

1. *The First Condition Is a Christ-centered Faith.* I do not know one of the really vital congregations which is not consciously and unapologetically Christ-centered. This criterion has nothing to do with either geography or denominational affiliation. Likewise, it is independent of educational levels, for it appears among the more privileged as well as among those without academic advantages. Almost everyone has noticed how the congregations lacking social distinction often outstrip the main-line churches.

When the day came in my own life that I realized that

I was an evangelical Christian without membership in any religious party, there came a new surge of power. One day I sat down and wrote the following, which still represents the clearest understanding I have of what Christian commitment means.

A Christian is a person who confesses that, amidst the manifold and confusing voices heard in the world, there is one Voice which supremely wins his full assent, uniting all his powers, intellectual and emotional, into a single pattern of self-giving. That Voice is Jesus Christ. A Christian not only believes *that* he was; he believes *in him* with all his heart and strength and mind. Christ appears to the Christian as the one stable point or fulcrum in all the relativities of history. Once the Christian has made this primary commitment, he still has perplexities; but he begins to know the joy of being used for a mighty purpose by which his little life is dignified.

I wrote these words fourteen years ago and used them as the conclusion of the first chapter of my most widely distributed book, *The Company of the Committed.*

2. *A Second Condition of Vitality Is Emphasis upon Ministry.* All Christians, if they are faithful, believe in worship; but this alone is shockingly insufficient. Much of the power of Christ lies in the way in which worship is supplemented by ministry, with its extension to the entire membership of the church. In many ways the crucial parable of the gospel is the acted one of the washing of the feet of Christ's followers (John 13:1–15). If we think carefully about this parable, we see in it a double revolution. It moves, in the first place, from mere priesthood to ministry, while, in the second place, it moves from the ministry of one to the ministry of all. Whenever a church sees itself not as an audience listening to a performance,

but as a society of ministers acting as a servant people in common life, new vitality normally emerges. Even worship takes on new and revolutionary significance if it is envisaged as preparation for ministry. The deep truth of this appears in the ancient Quaker remark to the effect that "the service begins when the meeting ends."

3. *A Third Condition of Vitality Is Emphasis upon Wholeness.* So long as Christians settle for either the personal gospel alone or the social gospel alone, they tend to decline in strength. The churches which are satisfied with stress on inner peace without action cannot go on very long, for their faith is fundamentally self-centered. One of the marks of the profundity of the spiritual insight of Abraham Lincoln was his recognition that personal assurance is not the center of our faith. On the other hand, if churches have only the social gospel, the time soon comes when even that cannot be sustained. It is strikingly true that the ecclesiastical establishments which have lost first the confidence and then the financial support of the rank and file of the members are those which stress the social gospel in isolation from evangelism and the nourishment of the life of devotion. But when both the roots and the fruits of the Christian life are emphasized equally the gospel does, indeed, become a source of power. All of the really vital churches I know encourage wholeness.

4. *A Fourth Condition of Vitality Is Intellectual.* I notice that the churches which are really alive are becoming little academies with a variety of educational opportunities being offered. A really strong church today will sometimes have as many as ten different classes going on every week, some being taught by pastors and some by others. Thus, there may be a class one evening in the Classics of Christian Devotion and one another evening in the History of Chris-

tianity. More and more it is recognized that Christians are not likely to perform their ministries in the world with any adequacy unless they think together, and they are not likely to think very well unless they read. At one period in the recent past the book table was a rarity, but today there is hardly a strong congregation without it.

The Christian is called repeatedly to a position of both realism and hope. There is much to make us sad; but there is, at the same time, much to make us rejoice.

CHRIST CENTERED FAITH
MINISTRY
WHOLENESS
INTELLECT

EVANGELISM / NOURISHMENT OF DEVOTION
SOCIAL GOSPEL

HOPE — JESUS RECONCILES
realism — man is a sinner

15

Greatness

March 1975

Because this letter is addressed to committed Christians my purpose is to share my deepest thinking about the nature of Christ's call in our lives. More and more I am convinced that the most revolutionary conception exhibited in Christ's words and practice is the servant idea. This idea stands in such contrast to what the world normally expects that it requires careful consideration. When the idea reaches people, however, it is sometimes extremely appealing. One evidence of this is the way in which four booklets on servanthood have been welcomed. Though the booklets have had no publisher in the ordinary sense, and though there has been no advertising, forty thousand of them have now been purchased and presumably read by several times that number of people. The booklets have been written by Robert Greenleaf, now of New Hampshire, who was one of the original Board members of the Yokefellow Movement twenty years ago. He is convinced that the servant idea is one which, providing it is understood and accepted, can change the world.

The clearest expression of the revolutionary Christian conception is found in Mark 10:42–45. The emphasis arose because of the perverse misunderstanding of the two apostolic brothers, James and John, who saw their discipleship as an opportunity for personal advancement. The key passage, which is as potent as it is brief, is transplanted by Barclay as follows:

> You know, . . . that those who have the prestige of ruling the Gentiles lord it over them, and that in their society the mark of greatness is the exercise of authority; but in your society the situation is very different. With you, if anyone wishes to be great, he must be your servant; and with you, if anyone wishes to hold the first place, he must be everyone's slave. Yes, indeed! For the Son of Man did not come to be served but to serve, and to give his life a ransom for many (*The New Testament* 1, *Gospels and Acts of the Apostles*).

Here is one of the most surprising ideas of the world. If taken seriously, of course, it literally turns the world upside down, as the early Christians were accused of doing (Acts 17:6). There has been, in the history of human thought, much emphasis on values; but here is something radically different, a transvaluation of values. What most men believe and act upon is directly challenged.

It is important to note that Christ does not reject the concept of greatness. Indeed, he specifically claims greatness for his movement and three times in Matthew 12 employs the vivid expression "Something greater is here." We are called to greatness rather than to mediocrity or triviality, but it is greatness with a difference. The supreme paradox is the recognition that greatness is expressed by the voluntary acceptance of the servant status.

When Christ refers to the Gentiles, he naturally refers not only to the leaders of imperial Rome, of which what we call Palestine was a constituent part, but to all the famous empires. The strange fact about these, including Egypt, Assyria, and Persia, is that each was built on the work of strong, proud men of the general stamp of Alexander. But all of them died. The church of Jesus Christ, by vivid contrast, was built on weak men. And it has survived!

After all of the intervening years, the way of life which Christ specifically renounced is still the common one. People in all countries seek prestige and power. Even in the church there is a power struggle and officers are given flattering titles such as "Your Grace" and "Your Holiness." But fortunately, we still have the shocking words of Christ, and they endure as a challenge to what we naturally seek for ourselves. There is much reason to believe that the most revolutionary sentence in all the world is "The Son of Man came not to be served but to serve."

We have noted, in other connections, that when Christ tells why he came, we do well to listen because, in every such instance, he is revealing his fundamental purpose. I was so reached by this at one time that I wrote a hymn in which each stanza is based upon one of the passages in which Christ says, "I came." Important as the other passages are, including that of John 10:10, there is good reason to conclude that Mark 10:45 is the most valuable of all.

Insofar as we truly accept the servant idea our lives are altered. The idea applies to every vocation, high or low. A follower of Christ is right to enter a business or a profession and to become as competent as he can be, but his competence is achieved primarily for others rather than for his own satisfaction. The Christian physician will, undoubtedly, have many rewards; but his chief purpose must always be his participation in what Dr. Schweitzer called "the fellowship of those who bear the mark of pain."

The Christian must develop mental powers, not for self-aggrandizement, but to lift as much as he can the burdens of his fellows. The Christian teacher is primarily interested not in his academic prestige and advancement, but in the clarification of the minds of the students whom he is permitted to serve. The mark of success in any profession, so far as the committed Christian is concerned, is not his personal reward but is the good that he can do.

The Christian conception of greatness will always seem strange to the world or even laughable and sentimental, but this must not deter us at all. We are marching to the music of another Master; and, though we do not wholly succeed, we know what the standard is. It is our most precious possession.

16

Difficulties

June 1975

In this particular letter it is my intention to deal with the mood which I sense wherever I have been during the past few months. What I sense is a general *unease* with a profound perplexity. Committed Christians appear to be as bewildered as are others. All feel the problems, but there is a distinct shortage of answers.

On the whole, people feel that they have been let down or even betrayed. Life hasn't turned out the way they expected that it would. High prices are encountered on every side, and there does not appear to be much real improvement in the economy. Though the citizens of some countries feel this more severely than do others, no part of the human family is really immune from the problem of inflation.

It is a fact that many institutions on which we have depended are in deep trouble. For those of us who have loved and admired the railroads, the bankruptcy of the Penn Central and the Rock Island railroads is a severe shock. If these go, what is secure? On a different level, we are hurt by the decline of the colleges, particularly of the Christian colleges. Some have ceased to be; and others, though they still operate, are essentially insolvent. In many of these both the moral and academic levels have, obviously, declined. The definitive marks of Christian higher education have already been lost in the majority of the church-related colleges. On the whole, the value of the degrees has declined.

The problem of welfare disturbs nearly everybody. Is the time really coming when half of the population will work to support the other half in idleness? What worries people is not the emphasis on compassion for the poor, which has always been part of the Christian message, but the acceptance of welfare as an expected way of life. When people expect this as a natural development, great damage is done to their characters. The wholesome self-respect which is necessary is almost impossible in a pattern of dependency.

The difficulty we encounter in providing enough physical energy is disturbing, partly because we have, for many years, assumed abundance. We should have realized long ago that fossil fuel is finite in amount and that we are in danger if we burn, in a short time, what took millions of years to produce. This is clearly a problem which will not go away. Undoubtedly we shall find new oil fields such as those discovered in the North Sea in recent times; but, whatever our discoveries, we cannot increase the amount under the land and under the oceans. The gasoline engine, a marvelous invention, has altered our entire way of life on the planet and has already depleted resources which will not be replaced. Clearly we have to learn to employ other forms of energy, such as those of the wind and sun; but the necessary steps will be neither easy nor cheap. In many ways, the party is over!

Almost everyone I know is worried over the problem of proliferation of government. In all parts of the world, government gets bigger and bigger and consequently more expensive. It is frightening to contemplate the size of staff maintained by each congressman, especially because there never seems to be a reduction. It is not surprising, therefore, that many thoughtful people compare our time to that of the decline of the Roman Empire. Will we, they ask, have to endure a new Dark Age before the emergence of a renaissance? Will the forces of decay have to run their course before a radical change can come?

It ought to be possible for committed Christians to speak redemptively to this situation. This is what the Christian faith exists to do; and we, unworthy as we may be, are its contemporary representatives. My conviction is that we do have something pertinent to say, and my purpose is to help you to say it.

Our first answer is that difficulties are not new. One of the reasons why the Bible is helpful in every generation is that it reflects difficulties on almost every page. It is not about people living in utopia! For a few weeks I have been employing the Psalms in my daily discipline of devotion, and I am struck by the fact that almost every Psalm speaks of the hardships of life. In the New Testament the reader soon realizes that the faith is maintained not in the absence of problems, but in the midst of them. Characteristic of the entire New Testament are the powerful words "We are troubled on every side, yet not distressed; we are perplexed, but not in despair" (2 Cor. 4:8).

The Christian knows that the good life is never easy. When, in the divine purpose, persons emerged, they brought a host of potential problems into existence, problems which do not appear in a prepersonal world. Stones are not afflicted with envy and covetousness. Clouds may be opaque, but they are never sinful; and they do not engage in the struggle for personal power. The difficulties which we encounter are chiefly those not of nature, but of human nature. Much of what we endure is the price of personhood, a price which we are willing to pay because a world of persons, even with all its problems, is far more magnificent than is a world of mere things. God has elected us as participants in the most difficult and most glorious drama that is conceivable. Christians are not surprised when they find that the human venture is not easy because they never expected that it would be so.

Our second answer to the prevailing unease is that God's grace persists. Of course our problems are not simple, and they never will be; but we are convinced that we do not face them alone. The more I meditate on the good news, the more I am drawn to the eighth chapter of Romans, the end of which may rightly be seen as the noblest of Christian creeds. The heart of our faith is expressed in Romans 8:28 with its magnificent statement of how God works in the world. This is one instance in which the Revised Standard Version helps us immensely. According to this version, with its fidelity to the oldest manuscripts, we affirm that "in everything" God works for good. We do not say that "all things work together for good," for they manifestly do not. There are terrible suffering and disease and sin, and these we must neither neglect nor deny. It is not *things* that are good, but God who works in them. God is not the author of tragedy, much of which is the consequence of human sin and self-seeking; but he can enter *into* the tragedy and *transform* it. This is the chief reason why the understanding Christian is neither a pessimist nor an optimist, but something far more profound than either of these.

Our third answer to unease is that of the record of history. It is historical fact that life can be lived nobly and even peacefully in spite of the prevailing storms. If we do have a new Dark Age, which we probably shall not, we can expect the Christian community to survive through the darkness as it once did before. The Christian fellowship endured when nearly all of natural science and much of the art of government were lost in the general decline. We know that it is possible to have the best thoughts in worst times. It is no accident that some of the best Christian literature has been created behind prison walls.

We are not part of a temporary movement, existing for a brief period and collapsing. Instead, we are part of something which Christ brought into the world with the prediction that it would prevail in spite of all dangers. He said when he first mentioned the church that the gates of hell would not prevail against it (Matt. 16:18).

If these three answers help you, first in maintaining your own faith and then in supporting the faith of others, I shall be forever grateful.

17

Russian Christians

September 1975

Having promised earlier to devote an entire quarterly letter to our visit with Russian Christians, I now welcome the opportunity to do so. My wife and I had long hoped to go to Russia because, without being there, we knew of the importance of that great country. There are only two major powers in the world, the United States and the USSR, and the prospect of world peace depends in great measure on the combined efforts of these two powerful nations. Although I know the importance of governmental relationships, I also know that individual citizens have responsibility in the making and keeping of peace. We must encourage Russians and Americans to visit each other and to go beyond mere tourism to a truly personal experience. In any case, I felt that we ought to go if ever the opportunity should arrive.

I knew that the best chance of a fruitful visit would probably come through the Baptist World Alliance. This is because nearly all of the people of Russia whom you and I would call Protestants are called Baptists in Russia. The Christians of evangelical conviction have come, increasingly, to unite under the Baptist banner with the consequent strength which comes from union. I saw that I could work with these people personally. Doors which are never open to the tourist might open to me. Fortunately, this is what occurred.

The story began a year ago, when four Russians came to Louisville to attend the meeting of the Executive Committee of the Baptist World Alliance, to which my wife and I were also invited. The Russian visitors heard me deliver a brief address and met us afterward. Thus, some basis of confidence was established. In December 1974 there arrived an official invitation asking us to be the guests, in June 1975, of the Union of Evangelical Christians-Baptists of USSR. This invitation was the document which enabled us to secure visas and to enter Russia without difficulty. The presence on June 9 of some of our hosts at the Moscow airport speeded our entrance so much that our suitcases were not even opened. We realized at once that the Baptist movement has come to be trusted as well as respected.

During our stay of two weeks we experienced generous hospitality on the part of Christians in four great cities, Moscow, Kishinev, Kiev, and Leningrad. These people arranged for our hotel accommodation and entertainment. They even took us to the Moscow Circus and, on the last night in Russia, to *Swan Lake*, produced by the Bolshoi Ballet in the Kremlin Palace Theatre. We traveled three times by sleeping car and once by air, each such trip being climaxed by a reception in the railway station or airport. Even late at night there appeared a delegation of local Christians bringing flowers and expressing goodwill. This was something which we did not expect and for which we continue to be grateful.

The religious situation in the USSR may be described rather simply. The state is officially atheist, and this is reflected in the mentality of the great majority of the people. All education is state controlled, and children are taught that the Christian faith is an anachronism, a relic of the prescientific age. Such is the unchallenged position of all of the universities. There is no counterpart of what we know as a Christian college. The existing church buildings are owned by the state, their use by religious groups being permitted in some cases, but never as a right and always with the possibility of closure. I met, in Kiev, with the chief government official concerned with religion and had a good opportunity to discuss such matters. Some of the former Orthodox Church buildings, including a few cathedrals, are active, but many others are closed or have been turned into museums. We went into both kinds, observing, in the active ones, a wedding, an infant baptism, and funeral preparations. These buildings do not have pews; the worshipers stood throughout the ceremonies. In one such building, where a special celebration was in progress, we did not remain because it was so crowded that there was hardly room even to stand. This, however, was exceptional.

The Orthodox Christians, who continue the tradition of the once established Church of Russia, are in the majority so far as the religious life is concerned. But there is no way of knowing how many Orthodox adherents there are. The Baptists are the second largest group, now numbering 500,000, half of them residing in the Ukraine. All members are mature Christians, none being under eighteen years of age. In addition, there are smaller numbers of Jews, Roman Catholics, and Lutherans. The Roman Catholic cathedral of Kiev, a very imposing structure, is closed, ostensibly for repairs.

The official position of the Russian government is that religious freedom is guaranteed to all persons. But it is very important to understand what this freedom means and what it does not mean. Religious groups are permitted to gather for public worship, but that is essentially the end of the matter. There can be no youth program, no Sunday School, no women's society, no church library, no radio program, no evangelism, no religious book store. Ordinarily, there can be no religious education; but there are at least two exceptions which we observed. One is the Orthodox Academy of Leningrad, devoted to the training of priests, and the other is the developing correspondence course for Baptist ministers, centered in the Moscow Baptist headquarters.

The severe limitation to one kind of freedom has had the effect, so far as evangelical Christians are concerned, of causing them to value the permitted opportunities intensely. They prize the fellowship partly because they pay a price for it. All committed Christians are automatically barred from membership in the Communist party, and their lives are always surrounded by danger. Some of those whom we came to know and love had earlier been imprisoned. The consequence is that the Christian fellowship means everything to these people. This is why there are no empty seats. In contrast to the Orthodox churches, the Baptist meetinghouses have seats; but in nearly every meeting we nevertheless saw hundreds standing in the aisles and listening through the open windows. Many of the members attend five times a week, each occasion lasting for more than two hours. In the time of worship there are several messages, much free prayer from the congregation, and many choir numbers. Attenders greet each other with kisses and address each other as brother or sister. Men and women are seated in separate sections.

Most of the attenders come on foot or by public transportation. In one congregation of eleven hundred members we were told that only fifteen own cars. For this reason there is no parking problem, such as is frequently experienced in America. The people work all day and then make their tedious trips to the meetinghouses in the evening with remarkable patience. On Sunday some stay all day, carrying their food with them. The evidence of both devotion and affection is almost overwhelming. Much of this is the consequence of being a minority in a generally alien environment.

Personal discipline is evident at all times. For example, every meal begins and ends with prayer, the people standing reverently. Many were interested in the Yokefellow disciplines. In one congregation eleven persons signified their decision to accept the fellowship of the Yoke, and pins have been sent to them already. Important developments may come from this.

The biggest insight which came to us in Russia was the recognition that we were witnessing something akin to early Christianity. Like early Christians, the people with whom we mingled for two weeks are living their faith in the midst of official opposition. One of the most surprising sentences of the Bible is that in which the apostle Paul tells the Christians at Philippi that he sends the greetings "especially of those in Caesar's household" (Phil. 4:22, RSV). Christian vitality had appeared in the most unlikely place. In the same fashion it is a surprise to find strong commitment in a country which makes no secret of its being officially atheist.

If we are at all wise we shall note this phenomenon with care. Above all, we must note what kind of dedication it is which can survive in such a setting. It is not mild religion, such as we so often observe in the West. Mild religion would be totally incapable of surviving in contemporary Russia. The only faith that is capable of survival is one which builds a very hot fire. Any other kind would go out and go out quickly.

Here is a valuable lesson for us. We do not have official opposition, but we are nevertheless surrounded by a mood which may be even harder to bear. For the most part, we have lost the vitality of Christian commitment which marked so many at the beginning of our country. On all sides we have the neopaganism that dominates the lives of the vast majority of our neighbors. Mild religion will never be able to provide a genuine antidote to the intellectual and cultural situation of our time. Our only hope lies in the effort to nourish a faith which is as important in our lives as is the faith of the Russian Christians today. They have given us a message of major significance.

18

The Way

December 1975

The responses to our September letter have been unusually numerous. I conclude that this is because the letter deals with a question on which many thoughtful people are really puzzled. Having heard conflicting reports about Christianity in Russia, they are eager to receive a firsthand report of what is actually experienced by Christian visitors to the Russian people. I am now convinced that there are many other puzzling questions about which we can help one another and to which we ought to direct our attention. One such is the relationship of the Christian to the non-Christian religions.

Though the relationship of Christianity to the other religions of the world has been a much-discussed topic from the beginning, it has become highly accentuated in our generation. There are several reasons for this, one of them being the ease of communication that makes all literate persons aware of the existence of others whose practices and convictions are markedly different from their own. Once only a minority of western scholars were familiar with Buddhism; but today millions know something about it, particularly in the form called Zen. Once Islam seemed like something far away and essentially limited to the Middle East; but now with the oil crisis a continuing reality, we are keenly aware of the importance (to us) of a faith very different from our own. For example, we are aware that Saudi Arabia, a nation in which no Christian society can be organized, is a significant factor in our own way of life. With the rise of Zionism it has become necessary for every thoughtful Christian to try to know what his right attitude is toward the Jewish community.

One common response to the altered situation is an evident weakening of Christian conviction. How do we know that we are right, many ask, when others are not in agreement with us? We cannot hold, simply, that we are right and all others are wrong. After all, there are many good elements in the non-Christian religions. There is much to admire in the Jewish homelife, and the practicing Buddhist can teach us a great deal about self-discipline. We soon learn enough of the manifest inadequacies of our own lives to realize that we cannot sit in judgment upon others, from a stance of superior righteousness. And, after all, it is required of us, even by our own standards, that we be tolerant.

The danger lies not in what has been expressed in the above paragraph, but in the next step that many now take. This is the step in which they conclude that one faith is as good as another. Absolute tolerance leads inevitably to absolute indifference. If one is as good as another, why should I bother to be faithful? Why should I be committed to Christ if Hinduism is just as good? The danger is accentuated by the use of a figure of speech which, if it is taken seriously, tends to undermine all intellectual effort. The world, we are told, is like a wheel that has many spokes, but each spoke goes to the same hub. If that is true it makes no real difference which spoke you follow. Or, to change the figure, there are many roads up the mountain, but each road eventually reaches the peak.

While the attitude just described is highly popular and even appears to be the mark of sophistication, it is important to realize that it is radically divergent from basic Christianity. The Christian faith has always held that, instead of there being many roads, there is only one! The Fourth Gospel, which is both the most mature and most spiritual of the accounts of Christ's life and teachings, is explicit on this crucial point. The embarrassingly clear words are, "I am the way, and the truth, and the life; no one comes to the Father, but by me" (John 14:6, RSV). Whatever this implies, it is diametrically opposed to the idea that one way is as good as another.

As a matter of fact, the commonly held idea that all religions teach fundamentally the same thing is simply not true. The more we study, the more we realize that the religions of the world are more marked by differences than by similarities. For example, most of the religions do not have a church, in the sense of a gathered community of those who support one another in preparation for their ministry to the world. There is really no church in Shinto or in Buddhism or in Hinduism and only a quasichurch in Islam, which eliminates women from the major fellowship of prayer. We take the gathered community for granted, not realizing how rare it is. The same is true of the participation of women in church life. The traveler, however, becomes keenly aware of this when he visits the Mosque of Omar in the Temple area of Jerusalem and observes that women, if present at public prayer, are required to sit behind a screen.

The truth is that, in our desire to be fair and tolerant, we have become sentimental. While we are highly critical of our own way of life, particularly of our religious life, we look at others through rose–colored glasses. We tend, in our admiration of Hinduism, to overlook the enormous price the people of India pay for the veneration of the cow. A little thought will make us realize that this veneration is almost wholly evil, measured by its effect on human welfare. Since, on the whole, the cows cannot be eaten, and since they eat much of the food which otherwise would be available to human beings, this is one of the chief causes of the food shortage in a dangerously overpopulated country.

Another crucial difference is that of the establishment of hospitals. These we take for granted as a natural part of our life, which Christians establish and support, but we look in vain for any genuine counterpart in most of the non-Christian religions. Some of the religions provide no rational support for the establishment of hospitals in that they minimize the importance of bodies. Christianity, by contrast, is concerned with bodies as an integral part of its faith. The Christian who has any true understanding of his position cares greatly about what happens to bodies. He knows that the Word became flesh (John 1:14).

There is a striking contrast between Christianity and the Eastern religions in that Christians have, in every generation, felt the need of intellectual defense of their faith, whereas the characteristic leaders of the Eastern religions have tended to be anti-intellectual. It is no accident that the Christian has founded many colleges because, as a follower of Christ, he knows that feeling alone is never sufficient.

The task of the thinking Christian is to achieve a solution which avoids, equally, the intolerance of one position and the sentimentality of another. It is not required of us to claim that the religions of the world are wholly without merit, for that would not be true. If there is anything that Christians can learn from other faiths, the right course is to learn it, for we need all of the help that we can get. If the Zen Buddhist can teach us to be still, that is something for which we can rightly thank God. But, at the same time, it is not required of us to claim that all faiths are equally true. This cannot be the case because there are many positions that are clearly matters of contradiction. It is not possible for both of two contradictory propositions to be true. If the equality of men and women is true, the denial of that equality is false, however appealing cultural relativism may appear.

It is possible to be tender without being soft, and it is likewise possible to be firm without being arrogant. God has undoubtedly reached out to his children in many generations and many cultures, but Christ's central claim remains true. The early Christians faced the same essential problem which we face, and they solved it by the powerful idea of Christ as the Eternal Word. This has been spoken to many in a variety of languages, but when genuine it has always been the same Word (i.e., the Eternal Christ). That is why there is only one Way.

19

Dark Age

March 1976

I have meditated for several weeks upon the topic of this particular letter, receiving help from many people. The topic is that of the possibility of a new Dark Age. Every literate person is aware of the darkness which settled upon Europe for half a millennium, obliterating many of the features of a once-splendid civilization. Rome, after centuries of brilliance, became the home of a few poor people surviving amidst the ruins of former splendor. Nearly all of science and technology were lost to be rediscovered later. Is there any real possibility that something like this will occur in the life of the West? A few weeks ago, at a conference establishing the chief features of the new Yokefellow Academy, McCormack Smyth sobered all present by saying, "We may be only one generation away from precipitate decline."

As all who know him are aware, McCormack Smyth is neither an alarmist nor one who is easily discouraged. He is fundamentally forward-looking, but he is also a realist, willing to face facts no matter how unpleasant they may be. In amplifying his remarks at the Yokefellow Institute, the Canadian thinker went on to say that what worried him most was the decay of a once-accepted set of values. He knows, as any thinking person knows, that there has always been murder and theft and rape; but his point is that, for generations, it was at least widely recognized that these were wrong. Now, with the almost total loss of the biblical set of values, there is the eclipse of the bad conscience. The burglar who breaks into a house where he slashes pictures, breaks china, and destroys other objects personally prized by the occupants does not even recognize that he has done wrong. By some twisted kind of logic, he thinks that he is getting even. Or, in the vulgar words of a song often produced in television commercials, he is doing "what he really wants to do." Self-expression is a poor substitute for an intelligent moral order!

It does not require much intelligence to see that, unless we change radically, the West will experience economic disaster. If we go on with enormous deficits running into billions of dollars each year, it is obvious that the time will come when the accumulated debt will exceed the total worth of the people. The worst part of this, morally, is that it is a way of cheating our children. When we spend more than we produce, we are harming not merely the present but, more importantly, the future.

However serious economic problems may be, they are fundamentally derivative. No economic order can survive except upon the basis of trust, and trust is a matter of moral values. If we decline radically, it will not be because we have failed to study economic theory or political science but because life has disintegrated at a deeper level. The sorrowful events reported in the news all stem from a deep sickness at the center. The bombing murders in a New York airport, the kidnappings in which enormous sums are demanded if harm to the innocent is to be avoided—these do not stand alone. They are merely vivid illustrations of a general trend that may be seen even in the daily stealing from department stores, a crime which raises the prices for all honest buyers. We can set up guards, but we can never watch everybody. No amount of technical skill can balance a lack of integrity or the absence of concern for human suffering.

In many sectors our moral laxity has contributed directly to economic problems. One obvious example is the high cost of security. What is especially strange is that this has added materially to the cost of education. And this cost is not confined to schools in the city slums. In what are supposed to be our best colleges, the expense of police protection is now a significant item in each annual budget. This is one of the reasons why tuition costs go higher and higher. Household expenses for ordinary citizens are increased by the cost of burglar alarms and other protective devices. In short, immorality is costly.

We all remember how, just a few years ago, economists stated confidently that the economy could be "fine-tuned," thus avoiding recessions and booms. Such academic naiveté is now universally recognized as silly because it did not work in practice. We still have both inflation and unemployment at alarming rates.

One of our chief points of danger is the cost of welfare. Every compassionate person and certainly every committed Christian has a deep concern for the poor, but now we are faced with something radically different. We have millions who feel no shame in being parasites, accepting, as their right, the support of the working population without any serious effort to join it. Every thoughtful person is bound to ask how large an extra burden can be carried by those who are productive. Clearly the time is conceivable when the burden of support will exceed the capacity of the productive population to handle it. This has already begun to occur in some parts of Great Britain, and results are disastrous. Thus we are now experiencing something of what McCormack Smyth says may be only a generation away.

By the Dark Age we normally mean the period of about six centuries between the collapse of the Roman Empire and the rise of the medieval culture. Life was insecure everywhere, somewhat as it now is in Lebanon. The closing of the American University in Beirut is a foretaste of what a new Dark Age would be. After the greatness of ancient Greece there came a period utterly discouraging to thought when survival was the chief concern for most people. There is a temptation to minimize danger by employing the sententious remark that people have always been worried, so why worry now? The trouble with this easy optimism is that what some have worried about has actually occurred. Crime has risen by 17 percent in Indiana in one year. Perhaps Gibbon's *Decline and Fall* should be required reading. Those who earlier saw the danger of a cut-flower civilization now have the sad satisfaction of observing that what they said thirty years ago has been verified in fact. Separated from their roots, many parts of our culture have already withered. The decline of the colleges, especially in moral tone, is one of the saddest parts of this verification.

We are called to face danger both realistically and redemptively. In faithfulness to the biblical heritage we remember that the noblest of the Hebrew prophets arose not in the days of prosperity under Solomon, but after the tragedy of the Babylonian captivity. In a similar way, the historian of ideas remembers that the Platonic Academy arose not in the relatively secure days of Pericles, but after the debacle of the war between Athens and Sparta. The day came, of course, when, after an existence of nine hundred years, Plato's Academy was closed. But that is not the end of the story. What is permanently significant to remember is that just as the academy was closing, Benedict was beginning his remarkable work. One of the bright lights came in the darkest time! It is something of a surprise to realize that Benedict and Justinian were contemporaries. Another contemporary was the philosopher Boethius (475–525). Boethius died in prison; but while in prison he wrote a remarkable book, *The Consolation of Philosophy*. Generations of readers have been helped by this good man's notable sentence "For this is sure and this is fixed by everlasting law, that naught that is brought to birth shall constant here abide." We are reminded, in this connection, of the classic words which meant so much to Abraham Lincoln, "This too will pass."

The Benedictine penetration of England in the cultural darkness after the Roman withdrawal has encouraged me deeply. It has encouraged me because here we are dealing with fact rather than with speculation. The Christian witness did not submit to the darkness, but provided an answer to it. Columba set up his tiny redemptive fellowship in Iona fourteen hundred years ago, and the amazing fact is that it finally penetrated the whole of Scotland. It is no wonder that the motto of the contemporary Iona Fellowship is "We shall rebuild."

We do not know whether there will actually be a new Dark Age or not, for the gift of prediction is not given to us. But we do know what the Christian strategy must be if real calamity comes. The Christian, if he understands his vocation, will always seek to keep a light burning in the midst of the darkness. He knows that it is possible to think the best thoughts in the worst times and that, if he is faithful, the morning will come.

20

Women

June 1976

The place of women in the Christian cause is so much in people's minds today that it is incumbent upon each of us to be able to provide reasonable answers to the questions that are asked insistently. Of the four thousand persons who receive this letter, I doubt if there is one who has failed to think seriously on the question of what the right place of women is, so far as the church is concerned. This is why we must try to help one another.

The importance of women in the historical development of Christianity is very great. Indeed, the Christian faith stands in sharp contrast to most religions in this regard. To this day there are religions in which women have almost no means of participation. In visiting the great mosques of Istanbul I have never seen a woman participating in public prayer. At first women had no part in Buddhism, though later they were included, particularly as nuns. By sharp contrast, Christ included women from the start. The evidence of this is abundant; an especially significant sentence is "The twelve were with him and also some women" (Luke 8:1–2, RSV).

Sensitive readers of the accounts of the crucifixion have long noticed how, standing by the cross, were three brave women, including Mary Magdalene. This same woman

came early to the tomb of Jesus and saw that the stone
that sealed the entrance had been removed. Likewise she
went to the disciples and reported, "I have seen the Lord."
In short, without the participation of women, the drama
of the death and resurrection of Christ would have been
strikingly different. The fact that women were not included in the twelve is not as significant as is the way in
which they were included in other fellowships.

So important were women in the infant churches that
we are driven to the conclusion that, without their assis-
tance, survival would not have occurred. In the church
at Philippi, the first on the continent of Europe, it seems
evident that the majority were women. In any case one
woman, Lydia, was the first member, and others are mentioned in the eloquent letter which the apostle Paul wrote
to the little group. When the term *Yokefellow,* an apparent
synonym for a practicing Christian, is employed by the
author, he actually gives the names of some of the women
members. These were Euodia and Syntyche. The words
that mean a great deal to many readers of this letter, words
that have given meaning to Christian discipleship, are as
follows: "I ask you also, true yokefellow, help these women,
for they have labored side by side with me in the gospel"
(Phil. 4:3, RSV). When we take these words seriously, as
we do, we cannot suppose that the earliest Christian
women were mere observers; they were involved in the
glorious enterprise as teammates. The words of Christ
"Take my yoke upon you" applied to all Christians, irres-
pective of sex. The word *Yokefellow* has no gender.

The highest point of the New Testament, in regard to
this question, comes in the remarkable realization that,
so far as the Christian faith is concerned, sex is not a crucial
factor at all. Sex is, of course, important in many other

ways; but when it comes to being committed to Jesus Christ, it is absolutely nothing. This is the revolutionary significance of the words "There is neither Jew nor Greek, there is neither slave nor free, there is neither male nor female; for you are all one in Christ Jesus" (Gal. 3:28, RSV). The apostle Paul put us in his debt in many ways but never more radically so than in this particular vision of greatness.

When the church was young and fighting for its very life, the women and the men fought side by side. Priscilla, whose name appears in three books of the New Testament, seems to have been involved as thoroughly as was Aquila. They had the good fortune to live before anyone had imposed upon the church a priestly system with its inevitable hierarchy. In those glorious days before the ecclesiastical system had become stereotyped, distinctions that later became important did not even exist. Women were in the total ministry because all were needed. Otherwise survival was not possible.

There have been many ups and downs in the intervening years. But today we are again in a situation in which, because survival is at stake, the involvement of women is a necessary element. We know that Christians are a minority of any population in any part of the world and that their enemies are strong. On every side we are surrounded by people who believe that God does not exist, some of these being in theological seminaries. Many of our neighbors believe that anything is permitted because they deny the existence not only of the living God but of any objective moral order. They think all values are matters of personal choice or preference. This is the real basis of the breakdown of sexual morality. If there is no objective moral order, why is not promiscuity as reasonable as chastity before marriage and fidelity within marriage?

If we face our situation honestly we know that we are in deep trouble. If help does not come through the church, it is hard to see where it may appear. Certainly it will not come from most of the colleges because they are part of the confusion rather than an answer to it. Some of the most vocal persons who deny ethical standards are themselves college professors.

The church is the one means of renewal on which it is most reasonable to depend, and this is true in spite of the fact that the church has so often failed to rise to its potential greatness. The very fact that the church is based upon Christ rather than upon human opinions makes a radical difference. We have something solid in bad times as well as good ones; consequently, we can weather serious storms. This is not a matter of speculation, but, being a matter of history, is likely to be repeated.

If, in our contemporary thinking, we combine our beginnings, our history, and our present predicament, we come out with a clear conclusion. Women belong to the Christian faith, and we need to take the fullest possible advantage of their potential contribution now! It is not enough to expect women to teach some classes of children, important as that work may be and is. We must encourage women to take real leadership in the growth of Christian thought.

Often I am asked where there is emerging a new Christian thinker comparable in stature to the late C. S. Lewis. Sorrowfully I admit that I find an answer difficult. I really do not see such a thinker on the horizon now. Has it occurred to you that the answer to the felt need may come from some women? Why not? Never once in forty years of teaching have I been able to guess correctly the sex of the writer of a paper if no name has been attached. I recognize no difference at all at this important level. Once we take down the barriers of false expectations, amazing results may come. In the words of 1 Corinthians 16:9, we can truly say that, though there are many adversaries, "a wide door for effective service has opened" (RSV). The intellectual emancipation of women may actually be the crucial step in ushering in one of the noblest chapters in the history of the Christian faith. There are many grounds of hope, but this is one of the most convincing.

21

Family Life

December 1976

The decay of family life is one of the saddest features of our contemporary civilization. That the change is drastic is understood by every person who tries to look at the world without rose-colored glasses. Hardly a week passes without each of us being shocked by news of the separation or divorce of couples whose life together had been supposed to be based on mutual affection and loyalty. To people who love the church, the news of familial disaster among pastors has been particularly upsetting. The failure of a pastor is not worse for himself, but it may be clearly more damaging for those around him. We naturally repeat to ourselves, "If they do this when the wood is green, what will happen when it is dry?" (Luke 23:31, RSV). If the spiritual leaders cannot make the grade, what is to be expected of the followers?

The breakup of married couples is more than matched by the growing practice of men and women living together without marriage and often with no intention of marriage. In some parts of the culture this practice has become standard rather than exceptional. It is often assumed, without argument, and apparently without doubt, that fornication is not a sin and really nothing wrong at all. With the invention of the pill having largely taken away the fear of unwanted pregnancy, there is now no reason for refusing to obey passing impulses. *This is because, for millions in the modern world, sexual experience is not looked upon as something involving principle.*

Anyone who has some acquaintance with the history of ideas realizes that sexual intercourse before marriage and infidelity in regard to marriage vows are by no means new in the world. There have always been individuals who believed in establishing connections outside of marriage, some of which have been firm, with evidence of mutual loyalty between the unmarried partners. The example of George Eliot and her male companion will come to mind, showing that extramarital connections are not always base or temporary. The same may be true in some phases of our present culture. Indeed, some couples engage in what used to be called "trial marriage," to be followed later by public vows, providing they prove to be compatible with one another. What they normally demonstrate, however, is a fundamental misunderstanding of marriage in a Christian context, in that they think of it as essentially a private matter. It is not a private matter because the community has a stake in the stability of marriage.

In a country such as Jamaica, where cohabitation without marriage is widespread, the major cause is poverty; the couples simply cannot afford to get married. In the United States, by contrast, the major causes for extramarital connections are philosophic. The problem amounts, in large measure, to one of belief or disbelief. Many have arrived at the conclusion that there are no objective values, and therefore no real right or wrong. They deny the fundamental position of Western philosophy, inaugurated by Socrates, that there is a real and objective right wholly independent of our opinions or wishes, which it is our duty to try to discover. If there is not an objective moral order, there is no serious reason for not indulging ourselves as we like without compunction. What people believe determines, in large measure, what they do.

The denial of an objective moral order has led to decay in many generations. That this position was well understood and practiced in the eighteenth century is the point of a famous essay in *The Adventurer* by Dr. Samuel Johnson. The sage used his essay to depict the philosophy of self-gratification and to show its logical consequences in society. Writing in the issue of March 3, 1753, Dr. Johnson makes his imaginary character say, of his own career, "It was not long before I disentangled myself from the shackles of religion, for I was determined to the pursuit of pleasure, which according to my notions consisted in the unrestrained and unlimited gratification of every passion and every appetite." This Johnsonian character, far from being obsolete, now seems exceedingly contemporary. Unless this philosophy can be changed, there is no permanent hope for our culture, no matter how clever we may be in mechanical achievements. The philosophy of self-gratification does not provide the basis for permanent society because it has within it the seeds of its own destruction.

From the time of Socrates to our own day there have, fortunately, been strong persons able to challenge the world view which now threatens to dominate. Among these the persons committed to Christ have been especially steadfast, and it is to such that I now address this letter. What we must do is to help one another know how to operate in a time of widespread confusion and decay. I think that my best service to my correspondents is to try to tell exactly where I stand personally and how I believe a Christian can respond to the ideological challenge. I see three ways in which, as committed Christians, we may respond intelligently to the current growth of familial instability.

A. *Realism.* We must never deny the seriousness of the situation. There is a temptation on the part of some of us to say that the problem is being exaggerated, that it will all come out right, and that there is no more of a threat to marriage now than there has always been. Comfortable as such words are, we must reject them as wishful thinking. Of course, there has always been sin, the Bible reporting much of it; but what is radically different now is that millions reject the very idea of sin and have no shame at all in what they are doing. They really believe that we are in a new age in which "all is permitted." The upholders of a standard are consequently seen as fossils. If we refuse to take this situation seriously we are simply hiding our heads in the sand, and no advance has ever come that way.

Part of the required realism is that we must not be deluded by the claim that the alternatives to marital fidelity are better or more beautiful. The sober truth is that they are not! The experiments conducted in alternative styles may begin with starry-eyed idealism; but, in the cases which we have observed, they end in sheer ugliness. In short, the Christian is called not only to affectionate understanding but also to realistic tough-mindedness.

B. *Clarity.* Even though we are outnumbered, it is our responsibility to state the moral standard clearly. As Christians of the biblical heritage, we believe in chastity and we believe in it unequivocally. It is our duty to say what chastity means. It refers not to a lack of desire, but to a life of self-control. That nearly all are tempted we do not deny; what we affirm is that God can give us the strength to resist temptation. By chastity we mean the rejection of sexual intercourse before and outside of marriage and the rejection of adultery within marriage. By marriage we mean a public commitment to lifelong fidelity as a sacred undertaking.

C. *Practice.* It is always possible, whatever the pressures, to demonstrate a standard. Christians have often been called to exhibit nonconformity, and they are called to this in the present predicament. Without self-righteousness, it is possible to maintain a minority ethic and to say firmly, "Here we stand." The best contribution we can make may be with our practice even more than with our doctrine. We have the marvelous privilege of following One who said, "For this reason a man shall leave his father and mother and be joined to his wife, and the two shall become one" (Matt. 19:5, RSV).

22

The Teaching Church

March 1977

The topic of this letter is one which is increasingly close to my own heart, "The Teaching Role of Christ's Church." The more I think, and the more I mingle with committed Christians, the more clearly I become convinced of what it is that is now most needed. Wherever we turn, both within the Christian community and outside it, there is obvious need of instruction, in that people do not even know what the gospel is.

We have long noted the biblical illiteracy at every level of the populace, including those who have had academic opportunities. Because thousands of supposed Christians are unable to recognize any biblical quotation or allusion, there is consequent spiritual impoverishment. In some congregations the gospel has been diminished to the mere art of self-fulfillment. Some current religious authors, far from emphasizing what it means to believe that God was in Christ reconciling the world unto himself, write chiefly of themselves. Egocentricity is all that is left when the objective truth about the revelation of Christ is lost or even obscured. In one recent religious book the pronoun *I* appears sixteen hundred times!

Part of the tragedy lies in the fact that, though seekers are, in many instances, prepared to hear a message of real

magnitude, it is not provided for them by those who have
the awesome responsibility of preaching to them. As we
observe this mournful situation, we turn to the words of
John Milton in his poem *Lycidas,* "The hungry sheep look
up, and are not fed." The fact that these immortal lines
were written 340 years ago makes no difference at all because the truth of a proposition is never dependent upon
the date at which it is uttered. We are simply experiencing
a recurrence of a malady which has been suffered before
and will be suffered again. The departure from basic Christianity is easy, having occurred many times in our history.
That it appeared very early in the church is the point of
departure of the apostle Paul in his letter to the Galatians.
"I am astonished," he wrote, "to find you turning so
quickly away from him who called you by grace, and following a different gospel. Not that it is in fact another
gospel; only there are persons who unsettle your minds
by trying to distort the gospel of Christ" (Gal. 1:6–7, NEB).

*What is most important for you and me is to realize that the
spiritual desolation is both a challenge and an opportunity for
the Christian who really believes something.* The emptiness is
so great and so evident that it determines, in large measure,
the nature of our own task. Ours is a time when the gospel
must be *taught.* Each one of us is now surrounded by vast
numbers of women and men who constitute a genuine
mission field. It is not that our neighbors have consciously
rejected the gospel; they have never heard it! They do
not really believe the tremendous news that God really
is, that he is *like Christ,* and that *he has a vocation* for every
son and daughter of earth. They have never been told
that God is actually reaching out to everyone who is made
in his image. They have heard of the Bible, but it is looked
upon as obsolete literature rather than something that can

speak to their condition here and now. They have heard the name of Christ, in profanity if in no other way, but it has never once been presented to their minds that he can be known in the present tense.

With an opportunity of such magnitude before it, the church of Jesus Christ must be redirected in its efforts and in its total ministry to the world. Those who guide the work of the church must know what the present need is and how to go about the task of meeting the need. Confusing as conduct may be, that is not the chief point of attack because the conduct arises from lack of convictions. The heart of the problem is what people believe or fail to believe, and this cannot be handled except by careful intellectual work, eventuating in sound teaching. There are, as the Scriptures say, many gifts, each of which is important. But different ones require emphasis at different times, depending upon the character of the dominant need. Once the need was that of social action, but times have changed so that what is now most required is conviction about objective truth. If people do not believe that there are genuine values, they can have no answer to those who preach "All is permitted."

Though the teaching ministry is what we must now emphasize, this is not new. When the word *pastor* is employed in the New Testament it is joined with the word *teacher* (Eph. 4:11). *Pastor* and *teacher* are not separated but constitute one category. The apostle Paul encouraged those who have the gift of teaching to employ it (Rom. 12:7). A pastor in the contemporary scene ought to visit the sick, but it is far more important that he should teach the seekers. The sorrowful truth is that, if he fails to do so, it probably will not be done at all. It may be true that no man is indispensable, but the good Christian teacher is nearly so.

Once we stress the teaching function of the ministry, we can see clearly the way in which the church must change. It must come, more and more, to resemble a seminary or a college. The local church can do something of what the Christian college was once founded to perform, but which, in the majority of instances, is now essentially a lost cause. With the evident decay of the college, someone must try to fill the ensuing vacuum. And what institution can do this better than the one founded by Christ, which has endured crises for so many centuries?

Fortunately, there are now a few pastors who see the new vision and have begun to put it into practice. One congregation in Colorado, with which we are in touch, now has a three-year seminary course with many of the same courses which we expect to have offered in a first-class academic institution. In one congregation in Oregon the Hebrew language is being taught with the purpose of helping members to understand the Old Testament. Why not? Do not the church women and men have the same kind of brains as do seminary students?

As the contemporary church begins more and more to resemble a good college, the library becomes more important; and the book table is operated by people who take seriously the ministry of the printed word. The membership becomes a genuine society of ministers in common life, each seeking the instruction required for his particular vocation. Many can become writers, helping one another to write better and thus to provide some of the literature that the modern world requires. The Sunday School will be seen as a start, but only a start, in this direction, for it will require tremendous expansion if the needs of the hour are to be met. Instruction one day or one hour a week will never suffice.

If the church is to be worthy of its divine origin, it dare not stand still but must always advance into new areas. In the recent past, we have made a significant step in stressing the *equipping ministry*. That is still a sound emphasis, but now another new vision is required. What we must demonstrate now is a ministry which teaches because it helps people to *think*.

23

Power of Ideas

June 1977

All of you who share this letter are committed to the kind of faith which can make a difference in the world. You are not concerned primarily with your personal welfare, though you rightly strive that your own life may be lived in conformity with the standards of Christ. You love our country and pray that it may be faithful to its high calling.

The topic of this particular letter is "The Ideas that Shape the American Mind." We know a great deal about the ideas which have shaped our life in the past, but we are not sure which ideas are dominant now. Many of us turn often to the words of Abraham Lincoln, first spoken 119 years ago this month. Lincoln began his famous address at Springfield on June 16, 1858, by saying, "If we could first know where we are, and whither we are tending, we could better judge what to do, and how to do it."

In trying honestly to know where we are, we face news both good and bad. That there is much to cause alarm is obvious to every thinking person. One feature of profound discouragement appears on the educational scene. This means a great deal to me because it is upon the educational front that I have spent most of my time and energy for most of my career. My college teaching began in North

127

Carolina exactly fifty years ago.

It was widely supposed that we were making a genuine step forward in our civilization when it was decided that the Federal government would use tax money to provide college students with easy loans. The argument was that this would turn out to be a wise investment by means of which the general level of knowledge and culture would be lifted. It has not turned out this way! Because in many institutions the general level of education has suffered a conspicuous decline, there is serious doubt whether we got what we set out to achieve. There are thousands now enrolled in colleges and universities who do little work of any kind and are consequently made worse rather than better by the expensive experiment. What is even more damaging, however, is the rate of default. Great numbers take the money provided by their fellow citizens and simply do not repay! At the moment, the total of the default is approaching the staggering sum of one billion dollars.

Naturally, there is now some effort, on the part of the government, to clamp down on defaulters; but there is no high probability of success in this effort whenever the persons involved are actually irresponsible. The major problem faced is not a technical one of finance but a deeply moral one. It is the ethical aspect of such a situation which is not only frightening but also revealing. We know a great deal about a people by noting the degree to which a sense of integrity is generally accepted. Whatever laws we create, we cannot get around the determination of people to cheat. The people who borrow and do not accept the responsibility to repay are not only harming those who made the loan possible but are undermining the general level of civilization. If there are those who default because of financial disaster, that is understandable though sorrowful; but it is far more sorrowful if there is an attitude of unconcern.

It is extremely naive to suppose that the chief problems of a society are technological. Technology, in the long run, depends not upon things but upon persons; and the reliability of persons depends upon their controlling beliefs. "As he thinketh in his heart, so is he" (Prov. 23:7). We are rightly worried about the depletion of our physical resources, particularly in the field of energy, but the depletion of our moral resources may be vastly more important. Intangibles make a nation.

One idea that clearly shapes the American mind now is that the main thing is to get money and to get it fast. We rightly love baseball because it is a good game, often marked by superlative skill in pitching, batting, and fielding; but it is being seriously undermined by emphasis upon money. The level of salaries demanded by some of the players is so shocking as to be almost unbelievable. However able a man may be in handling a bat, there is something ridiculous about his being paid $400,000 a year while his neighbor, who works at some less glamorous task, receives $10,000 for the same period. While recognizing that there will always be inequalities of reward in any economic system, this inequality is preposterous. No one is surprised if the wide publicity given by the media helps to make the ordinary citizen unhappy with his lot. Thus the emphasis on bloated incomes increases the general dissatisfaction and brings new inflationary pressure with consequent hardship for those of advanced years who live on fixed incomes.

The high-salary madness is by no means limited to professional athletics. Much restlessness has resulted from the publicity surrounding the granting of an annual salary of one million dollars to a woman newscaster. There may be some rational justification for inequality of this magnitude, but we have not heard of it. The average income of excellent pastors is only a fraction of what Congressmen now receive. Even though all, including the pastors, recognize that the work of the church is not undertaken for monetary reward, the glaring contrast is still ridiculous.

Somehow and somewhere there must be people who can directly challenge the money madness. If the philosophy of crude self-interest goes on unchecked, the result will finally be disaster. Who is more able to mount the challenge than the committed Christian? The Christian is in a strong position to be a nonconformist, partly because he inherits a long tradition of those who have been willing to stand against the world's values when those values are wrong.

We must let the world know that we march to the music of a different drummer. Whether there will ever be publicity for this or not, it is a fact that great numbers of Christians, while not claiming to be perfect, actually reject the principle of self-interest. In the past it has not been uncommon for professors in Christian colleges to teach for far less money than could be found elsewhere. Indeed, some have given their services wholly without salary, when they have had some other means of support for themselves and their families. Even today many of the lay officials of Christian movements spend almost as much time in Christian work as they spend in their secular tasks, but entirely without pay for the former. Because this is common, we often fail to note it as significant. But the time has now come when it must be mentioned.

We have many problems in our beloved country today, but it is very simplistic to suppose that they can be solved by economics. If the provision of money would suffice, our schools would be wonderful, for we have provided funds in abundance. Yet the major problems continue. It is frequently suggested that the problem of poor service in the postal system can be solved by new machines, but this is simply not the case. We all know that the best machines are inadequate if the people who use them are personally irresponsible.

The Christian faith exists to penetrate the world, and the chief way of penetration is that of providing a potent alternative to the philosophy of self-interest. This we do not need to create, for it already exists in the gospel.

Our task is to know where we stand and then to be firm, however obsolete our position may seem to appear. Since it is ideas that make our country, our responsibility in the dissemination and exemplification of Christian ideas is immense. A wide door for effective service is open, and there are many adversaries.

24

Maturity

September 1977

One way to maintain interest in these quarterly letters is to make sure that the topics treated are not monotonous. You will quickly note that the present letter is sharply different from those produced in the recent past. It deals not with some controversial problem but with the achievement of maturity, a topic which is bound to concern each one of us, providing we stay alive.

It has been almost fifty years since, as a very young man, I was first introduced to the famous essay of Robert Louis Stevenson entitled "Virginibus Puerisque." In all of the intervening time I have cherished his sentence "It is good to have been young in youth and, as years go on, to grow older."

Though the brilliant Scot, when he wrote these words, was only thirty-one, he had already attained a measure of maturity. Already he knew that things can be different without being better or worse, and he understood that "to travel deliberately through one's ages is to get the heart of a liberal education."

As one who has enjoyed both youth and middle age, I am glad to affirm that my retirement years have been the most rewarding of my entire life. During the eleven years since I retired from the professorship of philosophy at

Earlham, my life has been enriched by opportunities which could not have been possible apart from such retirement.

There has been marvelous freedom to do the things that could not have been done earlier, however delightful the earlier days were. My wife and I have, because of our freedom of movement, encircled the globe twice, employing many different means of transportation including freighters, land rovers, planes, and trains. It has been possible to give a full semester to Mount Holyoke College as a visiting professor, to live for eight months in Great Britain, to lecture in Greece and Turkey, to enjoy a speaking tour in Russia, and to visit former students in widely scattered areas.

The joys associated with these experiences are, in a peculiar sense, the joys of maturity. Long ago I read, in one of his *Ramblers*, the words of Dr. Samuel Johnson pointing to such a conclusion; but only in the recent past has there been a genuine verification of the truth of which the wise man wrote. "Vernal flowers," said Johnson, "however beautiful and gay, are only intended by nature as preparatives to autumn fruits." Only the end of a journey fully justifies the thought and effort which it entails.

What, specifically, are the autumn fruits which achieve such value? Among a multitude there are three that stand out with prominence. *The first is the vast accumulation of friendships* which maturity makes possible. In my own case, the friendships which I prize include those of my students and colleagues in the institutions which I have served. No week passes now without some renewal of such connections with my former associates in Guilford, Haverford, Stanford, and Earlham. When a member of my first class at Guilford loses his wife, I have time both to remember her and to write him a personal letter. A Haverford man asks me to visit him in Delaware; a Stanford woman writes to tell of her family; thirty-one years of Earlham friendships produce a constant succession of personal visits. Each one of these experiences enriches my own life, and for this I am profoundly grateful.

A second autumn fruit is the opportunity which maturity provides to engage in activities not normally possible during years of active employment or the care of young children. Entirely new studies can be undertaken, including the encounter with formerly unknown languages.

For some there is the actuality of a second vocation. The best illustration I know of the richness thus made possible is that of the career of the late Edith Hamilton. When we saw her for the last time—and she was ninety-four years old—we caught her reading the proof sheets of her introductions to the twenty-eight authentic *Dialogues of Plato*, which appear in the Bollingen Series. She told how, after her retirement from teaching in a school in Baltimore, she entered the wholly new career of literary production. The climax to her new vocation came when, on her ninetieth birthday, she was made the honorary citizen of Athens. Not all have the gifts of Edith Hamilton, but almost anyone can find retirement a door to some new chapter in life, however modest that chapter may be.

A third autumn fruit is connected with the written word. Many of us spend a great part of our lives accumulating books which we do not have sufficient time to read. There they sit, on the shelves, some of them untouched for months or even years. We long to enjoy these priceless treasures, but our lives are too full with urgent duties crowding upon our limited time. Then, in maturity, if we wish, we can savor the treasures!

I love my library now because I no longer read under the gun of professorial necessity. If I want to enjoy Robert Louis Stevenson again, and find out whether he is really as delightful as I formerly supposed he was, I can do so. There is no person and no duty to stop me. For most people this kind of freedom never comes except in mature years. Now I can peruse the works of thinkers, not because I am scheduled to lecture on Monday morning, but out of the sheer joy of encounter with some of the first-rate minds of the world.

Part of the joy of the freedom of perusal is that of looking at our own markings made in former years. Why did I underline this sentence of Carlyle's *Reminiscences* in 1925? What did I mean by this note in the margin of the *Theaetetus?* When I scratched that note, was that the first time that I really understood that philosophy begins in wonder? Did John Keats speak as vividly to me fifty years ago as he does now? Each day, as I look at the loved volumes again, I am grateful to the teacher who, long ago, suggested that I make my own index on the final blank pages of any book of value. By this means I relive, with conspicuous ease, the experiences of former years, but with added increments.

I am always a little shocked when someone says to me: "But you are not really retired." I hardly know how to answer such a remark. Of course I am not playing shuffle-board, but why should I? Since old age is the time of liberation, why should I submit to some new bondage? If some new production in the way of excellence is possible, why should I voluntarily reject it?

I keep thinking of the wisdom of Aristotle when he affirmed that happiness cannot be achieved in less than a complete lifetime. This means that the last chapter is just

as important as is any other. It is good to be young, and
it is also good to be old. Life is lived best if it is lived in
chapters, the point being to know in which chapter one
is and not to pine for what is not. I like my present chapter
immensely.

25

Evangelical Christianity

December 1977

Many thoughtful people are puzzled as they note the phenomenal rise of Evangelical Christianity, which is one of the visible marks of our particular age. Polls reveal that a large proportion of our people, regardless of denomination, think of themselves as "born again"; and the proportion seems to be on the increase. So important does this appear to media leaders that the National Broadcasting Network decided recently to deal with the phenomenon on three consecutive evenings in its widely viewed Nightly News. Because observers are surprised by the development, they are trying to understand how it has arisen and why it is so general. Perhaps it is your duty to help seekers to understand it. If I can help you, I shall try to do so.

The surprise now felt arises from the assumption that the spiritual phenomenon in question somehow represents a reversal of the accepted historical process. It has been widely supposed, especially among sophisticated observers, that the inevitable process of history is one in which people move from Fundamentalism to Liberalism and that this is the logical consequence of increased education. Now, however, the shocking situation is that Liberalism suddenly seems old-fashioned and impotent. The Liberal churches, especially those which have stressed social action and almost nothing else, are obviously growing weaker, while many of the churches which hold to a positive Christian belief are growing prodigiously. It is something of a revelation to see that the theological seminaries which once limited themselves almost wholly to preparation for social action are barely able to survive, while strongly evangelical seminaries, stressing conversion and mission, are in the healthiest condition which they have ever experienced. We need to inquire carefully if we are to understand a shift of such magnitude.

We are helped in our effort to understand if we try to see, first of all, what Evangelicalism means. It is not the same as evangelism, though the two terms are allied. Evangelism denotes a method of spreading the gospel, while Evangelicalism denotes a set of convictions. An evangelical might rightly be defined as a person, of any denomination or none, whose faith is Christ-centered. All of us try to be catholic, in the sense of being universal in our sympathies; but there is one word better than *catholic*—evangelical. The evangelical rejects "religion in general" which he recognizes as powerless, just as he rejects any faith which is merely formal or external. His religion is one of *power* because he has experienced the reality of Christ in his own inner life. A characteristic expression of the new vitality includes the use of a New Testament phrase about the power of God, especially in the words "the immeasurable greatness of his power in us who believe, according to the working of his great might which he accomplished in Christ" (Eph. 1:19–20, RSV). The evangelical Christian, as a direct result of commitment to Christ, being yoked with him and consequently with his fellow Christians, is no longer a mere churchgoer. He is liberated from the dullness which has afflicted much of the religion of the recent past.

The new power which emerges in a fellowship of those who really believe something and furthermore *experience* something is not difficult to understand. The deadness of some churches has been so great that almost any change is welcomed. If the change is one in which the formerly discouraged person finds fellowship with others who are likewise committed, the difference is one of kind rather than of degree. Surprising as it may seem, this is precisely what has occurred in the lives of several million people in our own generation.

The one passage in my autobiography, *While It Is Day*, which has drawn more attention from readers than has any other is that in chapter VI in which I tell of my own experience in suddenly realizing that I am an evangelical. The words I wrote were: "Without intending to do so, I had become an evangelical Christian" (p. 102). What helped me most was to come to the startling conclusion that "my one central certainty was the trustworthiness of Christ." I now believe that the amazing growth of evangelical Christianity thrives because it provides puzzled seekers with a solid answer.

Evangelicals are strong because they have moved from abstract religion to something manifestly concrete. They believe in the central role of Christ as Revealer and therefore Savior. Their deepest conviction is that God is like Christ, stressing the affirmation of Christ himself that "He that hath seen me hath seen the Father." Those who begin with a conviction of the Christlikeness of God still have many problems and they are not free from burdens; but they normally achieve, by means of the concreteness of their faith, a stability that is truly amazing.

What is emerging now is a spectrum in which Fundamentalism and Liberalism are the extremes, while Evangelicalism is the vital center. Naturally, the development involves dangers. Some who are termed evangelicals do indeed exhibit extreme forms of behavior, such as the excessive clapping of hands; but these do not represent the norm. A few engage in speaking in "unknown tongues," but they are the minority. All show emotion, as is perfectly right in a matter of such manifest importance for our lives; and a few show emotion that is excessive; but these do not represent the center. Part of the danger lies in the fact that those on the fringes attract undue attention.

We can now see that much of the success of the Yokefellow movement has arisen from the fact that, when it began, it represented an early form of the new Evangelicalism. For twenty-five years we have been stressing commitment as the central Christian experience. We have said, in season and out of season, that it is not necessary to choose between a Christ-centered faith and either intellectual integrity or devotion to the cause of justice. But we have always held that commitment to Christ is the place to start. With that as a beginning, both intellect and justice may be served. Without it no significant advancement of the kingdom of Christ is likely to occur.

26

Hope

March 1978

Though there are today some happy people, we do not live in a happy age. Millions admit that they have lost hope and feel trapped. Since they see no way out for themselves or for the nation, they can envisage no solution to their problems—financial, occupational, or matrimonial. All talk of a bright future sounds suddenly hollow as cynicism increases. The mistrust of all government grows as ordinary people realize that the largest single item in the family budget is that of taxes. Moreover, with constant inflation, the situation is not likely to get better.

The general mood now is that of a vague sense of disappointment. We are disappointed because many of the things on which we have habitually depended now appear to be undependable. One example of a major disappointment is that of our educational system. For years we have expressed an almost childlike faith in the redemptive power of education, with the consequence that we have been willing to spend prodigious amounts of money and energy upon schools at many different levels. It has been popular to say that if only we could spend enough, significant achievements would ensue. The sad fact of contemporary history, however, is that we *have* spent in fantastic amounts, but that our education, instead of demonstrating excellence, seems actually to decline.

That this is no subjective judgment is shown by the fact that scholastic aptitude tests have actually fallen 10 percent in ten years. After spending lavishly upon both buildings and salaries, our product proved to be untrustworthy. It is no wonder that many are dismayed and lose hope in everything. The tragedy is that where there is no hope there is no endeavor.

A second example of loss of hope concerns our economy, which, at one time, appeared to be the most stable in the world. Incomes are indeed far higher than they once were, but the strange development is that many persons find themselves in a worse economic situation than they knew before. It is reliably estimated that millions of families regularly spend more than they earn, even when their incomes are comparatively large. Since the anomaly is that of poverty in the midst of apparent affluence, it is no wonder that millions are today both confused and hopeless.

The more we study the matter, the more we are forced to conclude that even our financial problems are basically moral and spiritual. For example, one of the major sources of difficulty in family finance is the credit card. This presents a problem because the card enables people, if they will, to engage in temporary pleasure at the price of eventual disaster. The self-indulgent frequently employ credit cards with little or no thought of their essential dishonesty. One sorrowful result is dissension within families when the day of payment finally comes and funds are exhausted. Husband and wife blame each other, the frequent result being the destruction of family affection and solidarity. The important point to observe is that the tragedy comes not for economic but for moral reasons. Problems which appear to be economic ones are, therefore, ethical. The tremendous fact is that man cannot live by affluence alone.

Somehow the current mood has to be changed, and it is the vocation of Christians to try to change it. We understand the *malaise*, but we know that it need not be the end of the story. If people are discouraged because those things on which they have depended have proved to be unreliable, our marvelous opportunity is to tell them of that which *is* reliable. The living God is above all systems of education, economics, and culture. This is his world, and he will not let it go, even in spite of our stupidity and our failure. The ground of hope is not in our productions but in him!

The faith to which you and I are committed may rightly be seen as the most practical source of hope in the world because it is faith which produces hope. We begin to understand this crucial point as we study the holy Scriptures, noting especially the brave words of the apostle Paul, who lived in another age of general discouragement and who understood the nature of the answer: "May the God of hope fill you with all joy and peace in believing, so that by the power of the Holy Spirit you may abound in hope" (Rom. 15:13, RSV). Faith is necessary, but it is not just any faith that will suffice.

Life is not made good merely by the accumulation of possessions, for it is never good unless it involves a sense of meaning. Our hope as committed Christians lies not in what we have or in who we are but in *whose* we are. We are never condemned to the dead end of meaningless survival so long as we realize that we are called to be instruments of the divine purpose. For more than a quarter of a century I have turned repeatedly to the poetry of Stephen Vincent Benet, especially in the following words:

Life is not lost by dying! Life is lost
Minute by minute, day by dragging day,
In all the thousand, small, uncaring ways.

When I first saw these particular lines I understood better
than before where our major danger lies. The tragedy of
most lives consists, I suddenly realized, not in injustice
and not in the encounter with death but in hopeless, meaningless, and discouraged living.

If you and I have discovered any ground of hope in
life, it is incumbent upon us to share it with others wherever we meet them because we are called to "encourage
one another" (1 Thess. 5:11). Somewhere in the world there
should be a body of people who specialize in the production
of hope. Who are more likely to be candidates for this
role than those who are the followers of Jesus Christ? The
practical point of emphasis is that we, if we will, can be
the producers of hope. If you can spread some hope, you
may be doing a more important thing than if you create
wealth. We have an abundance of physical achievements,
but we are short on the intangibles; and it is intangibles
that support the world.

The conclusion of such thinking is that contemporary
Christians can play a crucial role in the recovery of genuine
civilization. We see this more clearly when we realize that
Christianity flowered first in a period when there was a
conspicuous loss of nerve. What good reason is there why
it may not do so again? Do not forget that we live to
serve and that the greatest gift which one person can give
to another is the gift of hope.